THIS BOOK BELONGS TO

24⁹⁹ Best!

#5301

A+++

A
CHRISTMAS
ANTHOLOGY

The Little Match Girl

A
CHRISTMAS
ANTHOLOGY

TIGER BOOKS INTERNATIONAL
LONDON

This edition published in 1994 by
Tiger Books International PLC, Twickenham, England.

© This arrangement of material Geddes & Grosset Ltd, 1994.

ISBN 1 85501 545 5

Printed in Slovenia.

CONTENTS

THE NIGHT BEFORE CHRISTMAS	7
THE OXEN	10
THE BIRTH OF CHRIST	11
THE PLUM-PUDDING DREAM	23
A CHRISTMAS TREE	25
SILENT NIGHT	50
HOW THE CAT KEPT CHRISTMAS	51
THE CAROL SINGERS	53
THE TWELVE DAYS OF CHRISTMAS	60
CHRISTMAS IS COMING	65
THE SNOW QUEEN	66
THE GIFT OF THE MAGI	104
A CHRISTMAS STORY	113
THE FIR-TREE	114
FRIENDSHIP	127
A CHRISTMAS MEMORY	128
CHRISTMAS WINDOWS	129
A CHRISTMAS VISITOR	130
THE CHRISTMAS DINNER	132
A CHRISTMAS SCRAPBOOK	142

CHRISTMAS MORNINGS	155
CHRISTMAS DAY	156
THE LITTLE MATCH-GIRL	157
CHRISTMAS DAY IN BUNNYLAND	161
NOW THRICE WELCOME CHRISTMAS	162
THE CHRISTMAS CUCKOO	164
THE HOLLY AND THE IVY	187
HARK! THE HERALD ANGELS SING	189
LETTING IN THE NEW YEAR	191

LIST OF ILLUSTRATIONS

The Birth of Christ   facing page 16

Christmas is Coming   facing page 65

The Snow Queen   facing page 80

The Gift of the Magi   facing page 112

A Christmas Story   facing page 113

A Christmas Memory   facing page 128

Christmas Windows   facing page 129

The Little Match-Girl   facing page 160
                                         and frontispiece

Christmas Day in Bunnyland   facing page 161

Letting in the New Year   facing page 177

THE NIGHT BEFORE CHRISTMAS

CLEMENT C. MOORE

TWAS the night before Christmas, when all
through the house
Not a creature was stirring, not even a mouse;
The stockings were hung by the chimney with care,
In hopes that St. Nicholas soon would be there;
The children were nestled all snug in their beds,
While visions of sugarplums danced in their heads;

And Mamma in her 'kerchief, and I in my cap,
Had just settled our brains for a long winter's nap;
When out on the lawn there arose such a clatter,
I sprang from the bed to see what was the matter.
Away to the window I flew like a flash,
Tore open the shutters and threw up the sash.

The moon, on the breast of the new-fallen snow,
Gave the lustre of midday to objects below,
When what to my wondering eyes should appear,
But a miniature sleigh, and eight tiny reindeer,
With a little old driver, so lively and quick,
I knew in a moment it must be St. Nick.

More rapid than eagles his coursers they came,
And he whistled and shouted, and called them by name;
"Now, Dasher! Now, Dancer! Now, Prancer and Vixen!
On, Comet! On, Cupid! On, Donner and Blitzen!
To the top of the porch! To the top of the wall!
Now, dash away! Dash away! Dash away all!"

As dry leaves that before the wild hurricane fly,
When they meet with an obstacle, mount to the sky;
So up to the housetop the coursers they flew,
With the sleigh full of toys, and St. Nicholas, too.

And then, in a twinkling, I heard on the roof
The prancing and pawing of each little hoof—
As I drew in my head, and was turning around,
Down the chimney! St. Nicholas came with a bound.

He was dressed all in fur, from his head to his foot,
And his clothes were all tarnished with ashes and soot;
A bundle of toys he had flung on his back,
And he looked like a pedlar just opening his pack.
His eyes—how they twinkled! His dimples, how merry!
His cheeks were like roses, his nose like a cherry!

His droll little mouth was drawn up like a bow,
And the beard of his chin was as white as the snow;
The stump of a pipe he held tight in his teeth,
And the smoke it encircled his head like a wreath;
He had a broad face and a little round belly
That shook, when he laughed, like a bowl full of jelly.

He was chubby and plump, a right jolly old elf,
And I laughed, when I saw him, in spite of myself;
A wink of his eye and a twist of his head,
Soon gave me to know I had nothing to dread;
He spoke not a word, but went straight to his work,
And filled all the stockings: then turned with a jerk,

And laying his finger aside of his nose,
And giving a nod, up the chimney he rose;
He sprang to his sleigh, to his team gave a whistle,
And away they all flew like the down of a thistle.
But I heard him exclaim, ere he drove out of sight,
"Happy Christmas to all, and to all a good night."

THE OXEN

THOMAS HARDY

CHRISTMAS EVE, and twelve of the clock.
    "Now they are all on their knees,"
An elder said as we sat in a flock
    By the embers in hearthside ease.

We pictured the meek mild creatures where
    They dwelt in their strawy pen,
Nor did it occur to one of us there
    To doubt they were kneeling then.

So fair a fancy few would weave
    In these years! Yet, I feel,
If someone said on Christmas Eve,
    "Come; see the oxen kneel

"In the lonely barton by yonder coomb
    Our childhood used to know,"
I should go with him in the gloom,
    Hoping it might be so.

THE BIRTH OF CHRIST

FROM THE GOSPEL OF ST LUKE
CHAPTER 2, VERSES 1–20

And it came to pass in those days, that there went out a decree from Caesar Augustus, that all the world should be taxed.

2 (And this taxing was first made when Cyrenius was governor of Syria.)

3 And all went to be taxed, every one into his own city.

4 And Joseph also went up from Galilee, out of the city of Nazareth, into Judaea, unto the city of David, which is called Bethlehem; (because he was of the house and lineage of David:)

5 To be taxed with Mary his espoused wife, being great with child.

6 And so it was, that, while they were there, the days were accomplished that she should be delivered.

7 And she brought forth her first-born son, and wrapped him in swaddling clothes, and laid him in a manger; because there was no room for them in the inn.

8 And there were in the same country shepherds abiding in the field, keeping watch over their flock by night.

9 And, lo, the angel of the Lord came upon them, and the glory of the Lord shone round about them: and they were sore afraid.

10 And the angel said unto them, Fear not: for, behold, I bring you good tidings of great joy, which shall be to all people.

11 For unto you is born this day in the city of David a Saviour, which is Christ the Lord.

12 And this shall be a sign unto you; Ye shall find the babe

wrapped in swaddling clothes, lying in a manger.

13 And suddenly there was with the angel a multitude of the heavenly host praising, God, and saying,

14 Glory to God in the highest, and on earth peace, good will toward men.

15 And it came to pass, as the angels were gone away from them into heaven, the shepherds said one to another, Let us now go even unto Bethlehem, and see this thing which is come to pass, which the Lord hath made known unto us.

16 And they came with haste and found Mary, and Joseph, and the babe lying in a manger.

17 And when they had seen it, they made known abroad the saying which was told them concerning this child.

18 And all they that heard it wondered at those things which were told them by the shepherds.

19 But Mary kept all these things, and pondered them in her heart.

20 And the shepherds returned, glorifying and praising God for all the things that they had heard and seen, as it was told unto them.

THE BOYHOOD OF JESUS

HUNDREDS OF YEARS had passed since the return of the Jews to their own land of Israel after weary years of captivity in Babylon, and they were still ruled by their enemies. A wicked king named Herod reigned in Jerusalem, and over Herod was the Roman Caesar. Yet the Jews hoped that one day a King of the Jews would be born belonging to their own Royal House of David.

Their learned men said that the Bible foretold that their King would be born in Bethlehem, but the Royal Family of David had long since left Bethlehem, and two of them, Joseph and Mary, lived as simple working people in the town of Nazareth. Still, the people had set their hearts on the coming of the King—a King who was to deliver them out of the hands of Herod and the Romans.

Now one night, on the hill-sides near Bethlehem, shepherds clothed in sheepskins kept watch over their sheep, in case wolves, or hyenas from the woods close by, should steal them. As they watched, they may have talked about whether it was really true that a great King was coming, or perhaps they discussed the number of strangers who had arrived that day in Bethlehem.

Caesar had sent a message that every man and woman was to return to the city to which his or her family belonged, so that a proper count might be taken.

So the people who lived away from Bethlehem had returned, and amongst them, as you can guess, came Joseph and Mary from their far-off home.

Joseph and Mary had indeed arrived so late that the inn was quite full, and the only place the innkeeper could offer them was one of the stalls which were generally used for the cattle and asses of travellers.

The shepherds, of course, knew nothing about Joseph and Mary, but in the midst of the night they were startled by seeing a strange light in the heavens, far brighter than the moon and the stars. An angel came floating through the air towards them, surrounded by all the glory of the Lord. They had never seen or imagined anything so wonderful as this beautiful angel, and they were terrified. But the angel said gently:

"Fear not; for, behold, I bring you good tidings of great joy, which shall be to all people. For unto you is born this day, in the City of David, a Saviour, which is Christ the Lord. And this shall be a sign unto you: Ye shall find the Babe wrapped in swaddling clothes, lying in a manger."

But now, even as the angel spoke, the sky was filled with more angels—thousands and tens of thousands of them—all bright and glorious, and they sang to heavenly music the wonderful song we sing at Christmas time:

"Glory to God in the highest, and on earth peace, good will towards men."

The shepherds watched in amazement, not daring to speak, and all too soon the angels' song ceased, and the heavenly host flew back to God, and all the land was silent again. Then the shepherds began to whisper together, and wondered whether what they had seen was real or only a dream. They decided that they had better go at once to Bethlehem, for if they could find a babe lying in a manger, then they would know that the angel vision was true, and that the King had really come.

Away down the hill-side they hastened, and knocked up the city watchman to open the gates for them. Then they hurried along the silent streets, until they reached the inn, which they knew by the lamp shining outside the door.

On telling the innkeeper their story, they were shown to the cattle-stall, and there, by the light, they knew that someone was awake. Probably there was a mat hanging across the entrance to the stall, and they pulled it aside and peeped in. There they found Joseph, and resting in one corner the young mother named Mary, and close beside her a little Baby.

Then the shepherds knew that the vision was real, for the Babe was lying in the manger, wrapped round with swaddling bands, just as the angel had said. For in that country babies are not dressed as ours are, but are wound round and round with strips of narrow cloth.

For the first moment Joseph and Mary would be startled at the arrival of the rough shepherds in the middle of the night; but when they heard the story of the angels, they knew that God had sent them. Mary, indeed, knew already that her little Baby was the King from Heaven; for, about a year before, an angel had come to her and told her that she was to be His mother.

The coming of the shepherds disturbed the other travellers, and the great news spread. for the shepherds went forth early in the morning shouting and praising God for what they had seen. The people in Bethlehem passed the news from one to another, and all who heard it wondered if it could be really true that the King of the Jews, and the Saviour of the world, had been born in a cattle-stall, and had a manger for His cradle.

THE GLAD NEWS SPREADS

Now in Jerusalem, which was only about six miles from Bethlehem, there lived an old man named Simeon. Year by year he had anxiously watched and waited, hoping that he would not die before the King came. No one had yet told him about the little Bethlehem Baby, but one day God whispered to Simeon, in his heart, that he must go that very morning to the Temple service.

The Temple was the Jews' church, and was very beautiful, being built of splendid marble, and great stones, and costly wood and gold. It was one of the most perfect build-

The Birth of Christ

ings in the world, and the Jews were very proud of it.

As Simeon went slowly up the marble steps, he wondered why God had told him to come. But as he stood still a moment, watching the people crowding to the service, he noticed a young woman carrying a baby, with a man at her side bearing two young pigeons in a basket.

This was no unusual sight, for at the morning service, whenever an eldest son was born, the parents brought him, when he was a month old, to the Temple to present him to God. If they were rich people, they brought a lamb as a thank-offering to God; but if they were not rich, then they brought two live pigeons. But now God whispered something to Simeon which made the old man's face brighten, and he hurried forward with the light of a great joy in his tired eyes.

We know who these people were, and what God told Simeon, and we can imagine how he hurried up to Mary, and asked that he might take the Holy Child in his arms. Mary was learning day by day what it meant to be the mother of the Son God, yet she was surprised at the old man's excitement.

But Simeon, taking the Child, stood trembling in the Temple Court, knowing that he held a King in his arms. Then lifted up his eyes to heaven, and said:

"Lord, now lettest thou thy servant depart in peace, according to thy word, for mine eyes have seen thy salvation."

And he proclaimed to all around that the Child had

come as a light to lighten all the nations, and as a special glory for God's chosen people, the Jews.

The worshippers began to gather round wonderingly, and amongst them was a good woman named Anna. She was nearly a hundred years old, and was on her way to the Women's Court. But she stopped and heard what Simeon said, for she also had been longing and praying that the King might come.

With what delight she now gazed at the Child, and explained to the people that the son of Mary of Bethlehem, of the seed of David, was indeed the King!

Presently Mary took back her Son, and she and Joseph went onwards to the Women's Court, which was as far as she's allowed by the Temple rules to go.

Then Joseph took the Child, whom he and Mary had named us, and went forward through the Men's Court to the priest, where he left his offering of the pigeons.

When the service was over, Joseph brought back the Child the waiting mother, and, putting them both on their faithful ass, took them quietly back to Bethlehem.

Joseph and Mary must have had a great deal to talk about that six miles' journey over the rough road; and how honoured they must have felt, to think that God had really trusted them to take charge of the Lord from Heaven! But Joseph and Mary did not boast of their precious treasure. They had found a home in Bethlehem, where they started quietly, watching the little Jesus grow in strength and beauty day by day.

THE THREE STRANGERS

The people in Jerusalem were surprised one day to notice a procession arrive at the Eastern gate, with camels and servants in attendance on three rich men, who had come a long journey from the lands towards the sunrise. Such important-looking people must surely have come to visit King Herod.

But as soon as the men descended from their camels they began asking:

"Where is He that is born King of the Jews? For we have seen His star in the East, and are come to worship Him."

"The King of the Jews?" the people muttered. "There is no King of the Jews." For many of them had already forgotten about the little Baby belonging to Joseph and Mary. But the Wise Men went on asking, as they were very surprised that no one seemed to know about this new King, and they were quite determined not to return to their own land until they had seen Him. So the question passed from one to another until it came to the ears of King Herod himself.

King Herod was exceedingly troubled that such a question should be asked. However, he called the chief priests and learned men together, and commanded them to tell him about this King whom they were expecting, and where He was supposed to be born. Then the priests told the king that God had written in their Bible that the King of the Jews was to be born in Bethlehem.

King Herod had never heard about the Baby Jesus, but he called the wise men, and treated them with great respect, and told them to go to Bethlehem and search diligently to find the Child. And if indeed they found a child of the Royal House of David, they were to bring him word, "so that", said he, "I may come to worship him also". But the wicked king did not mean to worship the new King, as you will hear.

The Wise Men set forth at once to Bethlehem; but how were they to know which house to enter?

Now, far away in their own land, they had seen a wonderful star, and God had told them that this star meant that a King of the Jews was born. As they travelled, the star guided them ever westwards; and now, as they left Jerusalem towards the evening, they found that the star was still there, and as they followed joyfully, it stayed just over the house where Jesus was.

How eagerly they entered! And when they saw the Baby King, they fell down and worshipped Him, and gave Him costly presents of gold and precious things, frankincense and myrrh.

It was too late that night to return to Jerusalem, so they stayed in Bethlehem; but as they slept, God warned them that they were on no account to return to Herod and tell him that they had found the King. So early next morning they set forth back to their own land. Then God spoke to Joseph in a dream and said:

"Arise, and take the young Child and His mother, and flee into Egypt, and be thou there until I bring thee word; for Herod will seek the young Child to destroy Him."

Joseph rose quickly, and, wakening Mary, told her that they must set forth at once on a long journey. He saddled the ass, and Mary hastily made her preparations; and through the night they hurried along the silent streets, and waked the watchman, that he might unbar the gate and let them go.

What a long journey it was into Egypt! Some of you will remember that it was the same journey that poor Joseph was taken when he was sold by his brothers to the traders; and it was the same journey that the old father Jacob took when Joseph, as the governor of Egypt, sent the wagons for him.

But meanwhile, in Jerusalem, King Herod waited anxiously for the Wise Men's return, for if they found the new King, he meant to send soldiers to kill Him. But the days passed, and at last a messenger told King Herod that the strangers had gone away back to their own country.

Then Herod was exceedingly angry, and in his wrath and fear he gave a terrible command. He sent soldiers to Bethlehem with orders that they were to enter the houses and kill every child of two years old or under.

Oh, what terrible sorrow there was in Bethlehem, as the soldiers came with their drawn swords and slew the poor innocent children! All the town was in grief, and the voices of the mothers could be heard shrieking and wailing in the streets, and no one could comfort them, because their dear little children were dead.

Yet all the time, the real King of the Jews was safe under the care of Joseph and Mary, travelling into the land of Egypt.

THE PLUM-PUDDING DREAM

I DREAMED a dream on Christmas Night
  Of a Hero stout and bold,
A gallant little English Lad,
  Who captured a pirates' Hold;
He captured the Hold! he slew the Chief,
  And loaded his Ship with gold.

He shipped the Gold, and shaped a Course
  For the gory Spanish Main;
Boarded the Plate-ship, sword in teeth,
  And hauled down the flag of Spain;
The proud Dons promptly walked the Plank,—
  As the dream cruised on again.

The dream cruised thro' a dark Forest
  Whereout there came a scream:
"St. George!" the Hero cried, "St. George!"
  And quick his Sword did gleam;
Six Paynims died, the Maid was saved,—
  Then onward went the dream.

The dream went on with Helm a-port,
    Till it struck an Indian trail;
The Hero said; "I'll have their Scalps,
    Sure as a ninepenny Nail";
He had their Scalps in Dead Man's gulch,—
    And again the dream set sail.

The dream set sail with Helm a-lee,
    Till the French fleet hove in sight;
Ten thousand line-of-battle Ships
    On a bowline, cleared for fight;
"I'll sink the lot," the Hero cried;
    So he sank the lot all right.

And still the Hero cruised and cruised
    Where Gold and Fights were rife;
With Spear and Gun, with Axe and Sword
    Men sought that Hero's life;
Yet Home he came, all Scars and Fame,
    And wedded the usual Wife.

On Christmas Night I dreamed that dream;
    But when the Morning came
No single word of it was True,—
    Which was a jolly shame;
For everything that Hero did
    I could have done the same!

A CHRISTMAS TREE

CHARLES DICKENS

I HAVE BEEN looking on, this evening, at a merry company of children assembled round that pretty German toy, a Christmas Tree. The tree was planted in the middle of a great round table, and towered high above our heads. It was brilliantly lighted by a multitude of little tapers; and everywhere sparkled and glittered with bright objects. There were rosy-cheeked dolls, hiding behind the green leaves; and there were real watches (with movable hands, at least, and an endless capacity of being wound up) dangling from innumerable twigs; there were French-polished tables, chairs, bedsteads, wardrobes, eight-day clocks, and various other articles of domestic furniture (wonderfully made, in tin, at Wolverhampton), perched among the boughs, as if in preparation for some fairy housekeeping; there were jolly, broad-faced little men, much more agreeable in appearance than many real men—and no wonder, for their heads took off, and showed them to be full of sugarplums; there were fiddles and drums; there were tambourines, books, work-boxes, paintboxes, sweetmeat-boxes, peepshow-boxes, and all kinds of boxes; there were trinkets for the elder girls, far brighter than any grownup gold or jewels; there were baskets and pincushions in all devices; there were guns, swords, and banners; there were witches standing in enchanted rings of pasteboard, to tell fortunes; there were teetotums, humming-tops, needle cases, penwipers, smelling-bottles, conversation-cards, bouquet-holders; real fruit, made artificially dazzling with gold leaf; imitation apples, pears, and walnuts, crammed with surprises; in short, as a pretty child, before me, delightedly whispered to another pretty child, her bosom friend, "There was everything, and more" This motley collection of odd objects, clustering on the tree like magic fruit, and flashing back the bright looks directed towards it on every side—some of the diamond eyes admiring it were hardly on a level with the table, and a few were languishing in timid wonder on the bosoms of pretty mothers, aunts, and nurses—made a lively realisation of the fancies of childhood; and set me thinking how all the trees that grow and all the things that come into existence on the earth, have their wild adornments at that well-remembered time

Being now at home again, and alone, the only person in the house awake, my thoughts are drawn back, by a fascination which I do not care to resist, to my own childhood I begin to consider, what do we all remember best upon the branches of the Christmas Tree of our own young Christmas days, by which we climbed to real life.

Straight, in the middle of the room, cramped in the freedom of its growth by no encircling walls or soon-reached ceiling, a shadowy tree arises; and, looking up into the dreamy brightness of its top—for I observed in this tree the singular property that it appears to grow downward towards the earth—I look into my youngest Christmas recollections!

All toys at first, I find. Up yonder, among the green holly and red berries, is the Tumbler with his hands in his pockets, who wouldn't lie down, but whenever he was put upon the floor, persisted in rolling his fat body about, until he rolled himself still and brought those lobster eyes of his to bear upon me—when I affected to laugh very much, but in my heart of hearts was extremely doubtful of him. Close beside him is that infernal snuffbox, out of which there sprang a demoniacal Counsellor in a black gown, with an obnoxious head of hair, and a red cloth mouth, wide open, who was not to be endured on any terms, but could not be put away either; for he used suddenly, in a highly magnified state, to fly out of Mammoth Snuffboxes in dreams, when least expected. Nor is the frog with cobbler's wax on his tail, far off; for there was no knowing where he wouldn't jump, and when he flew over the candle, and came upon one's hand with that spotted back—red on a green ground—he was horrible. The cardboard lady in a blue-silk skirt, who was stood up against the candlestick to dance, and whom I see on the same branch, was milder, and was beautiful; but I can't say as much for the larger cardboard man, who used to be hung against the wall and pulled by a string; there was a sinister expression in that nose of his; and when he got his legs round his neck (which he very often did), he was ghastly, and not a creature to be alone with.

When did that dreadful Mask first look at me? Who put it on, and why was I so frightened that the sight of it is an era in my life? It is not a hideous visage in itself; it is even meant to be droll; why then were its stolid features so intolerable? Surely not because it hid the wearer's face. An apron would have done as much; and though I should have preferred even the apron away, it would not have been absolutely insupportable, like the mask. Was it the immovability of the mask? The doll's face was immovable, but I was not afraid of *her*. Perhaps that fixed and set change coming over a real face, infused into my quickened heart some remote suggestion and dread of the universal change that is to come on ever; face, and make it still? Nothing reconciled me to it. No drummers, from whom proceeded a melancholy chirping on the turning of a handle; no regiment of soldiers, with a mute band, taken out of a box and fitted, one by one, upon a stiff and lazy little set of lazy-tongs; no old woman, made of wires and a brownpaper composition, cutting up a pie for two small children, could give me a permanent comfort, for a long time. Nor was it any satisfaction to be shown the Mask, and see that it was made of paper, or to have it locked up and be assured that no one wore it The mere recollection of that fixed face, the mere knowledge of its existence anywhere, was sufficient to wake me in the night all perspiration and horror, with, "O I know it's coming! O the mask!"

I never wondered what the dear old donkey with the panniers—there he is!—was made of, then! His hide was real to the touch, I recollect And the great black horse with the round red spots all over him—the horse that I could even get upon—I never wondered what had brought him to that strange condition, or thought that such a horse was not commonly seen at Newmarket. The four horses of no colour, next to him, that went into the wagon of cheeses, and could be taken out and stabled under the piano, appear to have bits of fur-tippet for their tails, and other bits for their manes, and to stand on pegs instead of legs, but it was not so when they were brought home for a Christmas present They were all right, then; neither was their harness unceremoniously nailed into their chests, as appears to be the case now. The tinkling works of the music-cart, I *did* find out, to be made of quill tooth-picks and wire; and I always thought that little Tumbler in shirt sleeves, perpetually swarming up one side of a wooden frame, and coming down, head foremost, on the other, rather a weak-minded person—though good-natured; but the Jacob's Ladder, next to him, made of little squares of red wood, that went flapping and clattering over one another, each developing a different picture, and the whole enlivened by small bells, was a mighty marvel and a great delight.

Ah! The Doll's House!—of which I was not proprietor, but where I visited I don't admire the Houses of Parliament half so much as that stone-fronted mansion with real glass windows, and door-steps, and a real balcony—greener than I ever see now, except at watering places; and even they afford but a poor imitation And though it did open all at once, the entire house-front (which was a blow, I admit, as cancelling the fiction of a staircase), it was but to shut it up again, and I could believe. Even open, there were three distinct rooms in it a sitting-room and bedroom, elegantly furnished, and best of all, a kitchen, with uncommonly soft fire-irons, a plentiful assortment of diminutive utensils—oh, the warming-pan!—and a tin man-cook in profile, who was always going to fry two fish. What Barmecide justice have I done to the noble feasts wherein the set of wooden platters figured, each with its own peculiar delicacy, as a ham or turkey, glued tight on to it, and garnished with something green, which I recollect as moss! Could all the Temperance Societies of these later days, united, give me such a tea-drinking as I have had through the means of yonder little set of blue crockery, which really would hold liquid (it ran out of the small wooden cask, I recollect, and tasted of matches), and which made tea, nectar. And if the two legs of the ineffectual little sugar-tongs did tumble over one another, and want purpose, like Punch's hands, what does it matter? And if I did once shriek out, as a poisoned child, and strike the fashionable company with consternation, by reason of having drunk a little tea-spoon, inadvertently dissolved in too hot tea, I was never the worst for it, except by a powder!

Upon the next branches of the tree, lower down, hard by the green roller and miniature gardening-tools, how thick the books begin to hang. Thin books, in themselves, at first, but many of them, and with deliciously smooth covers of bright red or green With fat black letters to be-gin with! 'A was an archer, and shot at a frog.' Of course he was He was an apple-pie also, and there he is! He was a good many things in his time, was A, and so were most of his friends, except X, who had so little versatility, that I never knew him to get beyond Xerxes or Xantippe—like Y, who was always confined to a Yacht or a Yew Tree; and Z condemned for ever to be a Zebra or a Zany But, now, the very tree itself changes, and becomes a bean-stalk—the marvellous bean-stalk up which Jack climbed to the Giant's house! And now, those dreadfully interest-ing, double-headed giants, with their clubs over their shoulders, begin to stride along the boughs in a perfect throng, dragging knights and ladies home for dinner by the hair of their heads. And Jack—how noble, with his sword of sharpness, and his shoes of swiftness! Again those old meditations come upon me as I gaze up at him; and I debate within myself whether there was more than one Jack (which I am loth to believe possible), or only one genuine original admirable Jack, who achieved all the recorded exploits.

Good for Christmas-time is the ruddy colour of the cloak, in which—the tree making a forest of itself for her to trip through, with her basket—Little Red Riding-Hood comes to me one Christmas Eve to give me information of the cruelty and treachery of that dissembling Wolf who ate her grandmother, without making any impression on his appetite, and then ate her, after making that ferocious joke about his teeth. She was my first love I felt that if I could have married Little Red Riding-Hood, I should have know perfect bliss. But, it was not to be; and there was nothing for it but to look out the Wolf in the Noah's Ark there, and put him late m the procession on the table, as a monster who was to be degraded. O the wonderful Noah's Ark! it was not found seaworthy when put in a washtub, and the animals were crammed in at the roof, and needed to have their legs well shaken down before they could be got in, even there—and then, ten to one but they began to tumble out at the door, which was but imperfectly fastened with a wire latch—but what was that against it! Consider the noble fly, a size or two smaller than the elephant the lady-bird, the butterfly—all triumphs of art! Consider the goose, whose feet were so small, and whose balance was so indifferent, that he usually tumbled forward, and knocked down all the animal creation. Consider Noah and his family, like idiotic tobacco-stoppers; and how the leopard stuck to warm little fingers; and how the tails of the larger animals used gradually to resolve themselves into frayed bits of string!

Hush! Again a forest, and somebody up in a tree—not Robin Hood, not Valentine, not the Yellow Dwarf (I have passed him and all Mother Bunch's wonders, without mention), but an Eastern King with a glittering scimitar and turban. By Allah! two Eastern Kings, for I see another, looking over his shoulder! Down upon the grass, at the tree's foot, lies the full length of a coal-black Giant, stretched asleep, with his head in a lady's lap; and near them is a glass box, fastened with four locks of shining steel, in which he keeps the lady prisoner when he is awake. I see the four keys at his girdle now. The lady makes signs to the two kings in the tree, who softly descend It is the setting-in of the bright Arabian Nights.

Oh, now all common things become uncommon and enchanted to me. All lamps are wonderful; all rings are talismans Common flowerpots are full of treasure, with a little earth scattered on the top; trees are for Ali Baba to hide in; beef-steaks are to throw down into the Valley of Diamonds, that the precious stones may stick to them, and be carried by the eagles to their nests, whence the traders, with loud cries, will scare them Tarts are made, according to the recipe of the Vizier's son of Bussorah, who turned pastrycook after he was set down in his drawers at the gate of Damascus; cobblers are all Mustaphas, and in the habit of sewing up people cut in four pieces, to whom they are taken blindfold.

Any iron ring let into stone is the entrance to a cave which only waits for the magician, and the little fire, and the necromancy, that will make the earth shake. All the dates imported come from the same tree as that unlucky date, with whose shell the merchant knocked out the eye of the genie's invisible son. All olives are of the stock of that fresh fruit, concerning which the Commander of the Faithful overheard the boy conduct the fictitious trial of the fraudulent olive merchant; all apples are akin to the apple purchased (with two others' from the Sultan's gardener for three sequins, and which the tall black slave stole from the child. All dogs are associated with the dog, really a transformed man, who jumped upon the baker's counter, and put his paw on the piece of bad money. All rice recalls the rice which the awful lady, who was a ghoul, could only peck by grains, because of her nightly feasts in the burial-place. My very rocking-horse—there he is, with his nostrils turned completely inside-out, indicative of Blood!—should have a peg in his neck, by virtue thereof to fly away with me, as the wooden horse did with the Prince of Persia, in the sight of all his father's court.

Yes, on every object that I recognise among those upper branches of my Christmas Tree, I see this fairy light! When I wake in bed, at daybreak, on the cold, dark, winter mornings, the white snow dimly beheld, outside, through the frost on the windowpane, I hear Dinarzade. "Sister, sister, if you are yet awake, I pray you finish the history of the Young King of the Black Islands." Scheherazade replies, "If my lord the Sultan will suffer me to live another day, sister, I will not only finish that, but tell you a more wonderful story yet." Then, the gracious Sultan goes out, giving no orders for the execution, and we all three breathe again.

At this height of my tree I begin to see, cowering among the leaves—it may be born of turkey, or of pudding, or mince pie, or of these many fancies, jumbled with Robinson Crusoe on his desert island, Phillip Quarll among the monkeys, Sandford and Merton with Mr. Barlow, Mother Bunch, and the Mask—or it may be the result of indigestion, assisted by imagination and over-doctoring—a prodigious nightmare. It is so exceedingly indistinct, that I don't know why it's frightful—but I know it is. I can only make out that it is an immense array of shapeless things, which appear to be planted on a vast exaggeration of the lazy-tongs that used to bear the toy soldiers, and to be slowly coming close to my eyes, and receding to an immeasurable distance When it comes closest, it is worse. In connection with it I descry remembrances of winter nights incredibly long; of being sent early to bed, as a punishment for some small offence, and waking in two hours, with a sensation of having been asleep two nights; of the laden hopelessness of morning ever dawning; and the oppression of a weight of remorse.

And now, I see a wonderful row of little lights rise smoothly out of the ground, before a vast green curtain. Now, a bell rings—a magic bell, which still sounds in my ears unlike all other bells—and music plays, amidst a buzz of voices, and a fragrant smell of orange peel and oil. Anon, the magic bell commands the music to cease, and the great green curtain rolls itself up majestically, and The Play begins! The devoted dog of Montargis avenges the death of his master, foully murdered in the Forest of Bondy; and a humorous Peasant with a red nose and a very little hat, whom I take from this hour forth to my bosom as a friend (I think he was a Waiter or an Hostler at a village Inn, but many years have passed since he and I have met), remarks that the sassigassity of that dog is indeed surprising; and evermore this jocular conceit will live in my remembrance fresh and unfading, over-topping all possible jokes, unto the end of time. Or now, I learn with bitter tears how poor Jane Shore, dressed all in white, and with her brown hair hanging down, went starving through the streets; or how George Barnwell killed the worthiest uncle that man ever had, and was afterwards so sorry for it that he ought to have been let off Comes swift to comfort me, the Pantomime—stupendous Phenomenon!—when clowns are shot from loaded mortars into the great chandelier, bright constellation that it is; when Harlequins, covered all over with scales of pure gold, twist and sparkle, like amazing fish; when Pantaloon (whom I deem it no irreverence to compare in my own mind to my grandfather) puts red-hot pokers in his pocket, and cries "Here's somebody coming!" or taxes the Clown with petty larceny, by saying, "Now, I sawed you do it!" when Everything is capable, with the greatest of ease, of being changed into Anything; and "Nothing is, but thinking makes it so." Now, too, I perceive my first experience of the dreary sensation—often to return in after-life—of being unable, next day, to get back to the cull, settled world; of wanting to live in the bright atmosphere I have quitted; of doting on the little Fairy, with a wand like a celestial Barber's Pole, and pining for a Fairy immortality along with her. Ah, she comes back in many shapes, as my eye wanders down the branches of my Christmas Tree, and goes as often, and has never yet stayed by me!

Out of this delight springs the toy-theatre—there it is, with its familiar proscenium, and ladies in feathers, in the boxes!—and all its attendant occupation with paste and glue, and gum, and water colours, in the getting-up of the Miller and his Men, and Elizabeth, or the Exile of Siberia. In spite of a few besetting accidents and failures (particularly, an unreasonable disposition in the respectable Kelmar, and some others, to become faint in the legs, and double up, at exciting points of the drama), a teeming world of fancies so suggestive and all-embracing, that, far below it on my Christmas Tree, I see dark, dirty, real Theatres in the daytime, adorned with these associations as with the freshest garlands of the rarest flowers, and charming me yet.

But hark! The Waits are playing, and they break my childish sleep! What images do I associate with the Christmas music as I see them set forth on the Christmas

Tree? Known before all the others, keeping far apart from all the others, they gather round my little bed. An angel, speaking to a group of shepherds in a field; some travellers, with eyes uplifted, following a star; a baby in a manger; a child in a spacious temple, talking with grave men; a solemn figure, with a mild and beautiful face, raising a dead girl by the hand; again, near a city gate, calling back the son of a widow, on his bier, to life; a crowd of people looking through the open roof of the chamber where he sits, and letting down a sick person on a bed, with ropes; the same, in a tempest, walking on the water to a ship; again, on a sea-shore, teaching a great multitude again, with a child upon his knee, and other children round; again restoring sight to the blind, speech to the dumb, hearing to the deaf, health to the sick, strength to the lame, knowledge to the ignorant again, dying upon a Cross, watched by armed soldiers, a thick darkness coming on, the earth beginning to shake, and only one voice heard 'Forgive them, for they know not what they do'

Still, on the lower and maturer branches of the Tree, Christmas associations cluster thick School-books shut up; Ovid and Virgil silenced; the Rule of Three, with its cool impertinent inquiries, long disposed of; Terence and Plautus acted no more, in an arena of huddle desks and forms, all chipped, and notched, and inked; trodden grass and the softened noise of shouts in the evening air; the tree is still fresh, still gay. If I no more come home at Christmas-time, there will be boys and girls (thank

Heaven!) while the world lasts; and they do! Yonder they dance and play upon the branches of my Tree, God bless them, merrily, and my heart dances and plays too!

And I *do* come home at Christmas. We all do, or we all should We all come home, or ought to come home for a short holiday—the longer the better—from the great boarding-school, where we are for ever working at our arithmetical slates, to take, and give a rest. As to going a-visiting, where can we not go, if we will; where have we not been, when we would; starting our fancy from our Christmas Tree!

Away into the winter prospect. There are many such upon the tree! On, by low-lying, misty grounds, through fens and fogs, up long hills, winding dark as caverns between thick plantations, almost shutting out the sparkling stars; so, out on broad heights, until we stop at last, with sudden silence at an avenue. The gate-bell has a deep, half-awful sound in the frosty air; the gate swings open on its hinges; and, as we drive up to the great house, the glancing lights grow larger in the windows, and the opposing, rows of trees seem to fall solemnly back on either side, to give us place. At intervals, all day, a frightened hare has shot across this whitened turf; or the distant clatter of a herd of deer trampling the hard frost, has, for the moment, crushed the silence too. Their watchful eyes beneath the fern may be shining now, if we could see them, like the ice dewdrops on the leaves; but they are still, and all is still. And so, the lights growing larger, and the trees falling back before us, and closing up again behind us, as if to forbid retreat, we come to the house.

There is probably a smell of roast chestnuts and other good comfortable things all the time, for we are telling Winter Stories—Ghost Stories, or more shame for us—round the Christmas fire; and we have never stirred except to draw a little nearer to it. But, no matter for that. We came to the house, and it is an old house, full of great chimneys where wood is burnt on ancient dogs upon the hearth, and grim portraits (some of them with grim legends, too) lower distrustfully from the oaken panels of the walls We are a middle-aged nobleman, and we make a generous supper with our host and hostess and their guests—it being Christmas-time, and the old house full of company—and then we go to bed. Our room is a very old room. It is hung with tapestry We don't like the portrait of the cavalier in green, over the fire-place. There are great black beams in the ceiling, and there is a great black bedstead, supported at the foot by two great black figures, who seem to have come off a couple of tombs in the old baronial church in the park, for our particular accommodation. But, we are not a superstitious nobleman, and we do not mind. Well! we dismiss our servants lock the door, and sit before the fire in our dressing-gown, musing about a great many things. At length we go to bed. Well! we can't sleep. We toss and tumble, and can't sleep. The embers on the hearth burn fitfully and make the room look ghostly. We can't help peeping out over the counterpane, at the two black figures and the cavalier—that wicked-looking cavalier—in green. In the flickering light they seem to advance and retire which, though we are not by any means a superstitious nobleman, is not agreeable.

Well! we get nervous—more and more nervous. We say "This is very foolish, but we can't stand this; we'll pretend to be ill, and knock up somebody." Well! we are just going to do it, when the locked door opens, and there comes in a young woman, deadly pale, and with long fair hair, who glides to the fire, and sits down in the chair we have left there, wringing her hands. Then we notice that her clothes are wet. Our tongue cleaves to the roof of our mouth, and we can but we observe her accurately. Her clothes are wet; her long hair is dabbled with moist mud; she is dressed in the fashion of two years ago; and she has at her girdle a rusty bunch of keys. Well! there she sits, and we can't even faint, we are in such a state about it. Presently she gets up, and tries all the locks in the room with the rusty keys, which won't fit one of them; then, she fixes her eyes on the portrait of the cavalier in green, and says, in a low, terrible voice, "The stags know it!" After that, she wrings her hands again, passes the bedside and goes out at the door We hurry on our dressing-gown seize our pistols (we always travel with pistols), and are following when we find the door locked. We turn the key, look out into the gallery; no one there. We wander away and try to find our servant. Can't be done. We pace the gallery till daybreak; then return to our deserted room, fall asleep, and are awakened by our servant (nothing ever haunts *him*) and the shining sun. Well! we make a wretched breakfast, and all the company say we look queer.

After breakfast, we go over the house with our host, and then we take him to the portrait of the cavalier in green, and then it all comes out. He was false to a young house-keeper once attached to the family, and famous for her beauty, who drowned herself in a pond, and whose body was discovered after a long time, because the stags refused to drink of the water. Since which, it has been whispered that she traverses the house at midnight (but goes especially to that room where the cavalier was wont to sleep), trying the old locks with the rusty keys. Well! we tell our host of what we have seen, and a shade comes over his features, and he begs it may be hushed up; and so it is. But, it's all true; and we said so, before we died (we are dead now) to many responsible people

There is no end to the old houses, with resounding galleries and dismal state-chambers, and haunted wings shut up for many years, through which we may ramble with an agreeable creeping up our back, and encounter any number of ghosts, but (it is worthy of remark perhaps) reducible to a very few general types and classes; for, ghosts have little originality, and 'walk' in a beaten track. Thus, it comes to pass, that a certain room in a certain old hall, where a certain bad lord, baronet, knight, or gentleman, shot himself, has certain planks in the floor from

which the blood *will* not be taken out. You may scrape
and scrape, as the present owner has done, or plane and
plane, as his father did, or scrub and scrub as his grandfather did, or burn and burn with strong acids as his great-
grandfather did, but there the blood will still be—no red-
der and no paler—no more and no less—always just the
same. Thus, in such another house there is a haunted
door, that never will keep open; or another door that
never will keep shut; or a haunted sound of a spinning
wheel, or a hammer, or a footstep, or a cry, or a sigh, or a
horse's tramp, or the rattling of a chain. Or else, there is a
turret-clock, which, at the midnight hour, strikes thirteen
when the head of the family is going to die; or a shadowy,
immovable black carriage which at such a time is always
seen by somebody, waiting near the great gates in the sta-
ble-yard. Or thus, it came to pass how Lady Mary went to
pay a visit at a large wild house in the Scottish Highlands,
and, being fatigued with her long journey, retired to bed
early, and innocently said, next morning, at the breakfast
table, "How odd, to have so late a party last night, in this
remote place, and not to tell me of it, before I went to
bed!" Then, every one asked Lady Mary what she meant?
Then, Lady Mary replied, "Why, all night long, the carriages were driving round and round the terrace, under-
neath my window!" Then, the owner of the house turned
pale, and so did his Lady, and Charles Macdoodle of
Macdoodle signed to Lady Mary to say no more, and everyone was silent. After breakfast, Charles Macdoodle told

Lady Mary that it was a tradition in the family that those rumbling carriages on the terrace betokened death. And so it proved, for, two months afterwards the Lady of the mansion died. And Lady Mary, who was a Maid of Honour at Court, often told this story to the old Queen Charlotte; by this token that the old King always said, "Eh, eh? what, what? Ghosts, ghosts? No such thing, no such thing!" And never left off saying so, until he went to bed.

Or, a friend of somebody's whom most of us know, when he was a young man at college, had a particular friend, with whom he made the compact that, if it were possible for the Spirit to return to this earth after its separation from the body, he of the twain who first died, should reappear to the other. In the course of time, this compact was forgotten by our friend; the two young men having progressed in life, and taking diverging paths that were wide asunder. But, one night, many years afterwards, our friend being in the North of England, and staying for the night in an inn, on the Yorkshire Moors, happened to look out of bed; and there, in the moonlight, leaning on a bureau near the window, steadfastly regarding him, saw his old college friend! The appearance being solemnly addressed, replied, in a kind of whisper, but very audibly "Do not come near me, I am dead I am here to redeem my promise I come from another world, but may not disclose its secrets!" Then, the whole form becoming paler, melted, as it were, into the moonlight, and faded away.

Or, there was the daughter of the first occupier of the picturesque Elizabethan house, so famous in our neighbourhood. You have heard about her? No! why, She went out one summer evening at twilight, when she was a beautiful girl, just seventeen years of age, to gather flowers in the garden; and presently came running, terrified, into the hall to her father, saying, "Oh, dear father, I have met myself!" He took her in his arms, and told her it was fancy, but she said, "Oh, no! I met myself in the broad walk, and I was pale and gathering withered flowers, and I turned my head, and held them up!" And, that night, she died; and a picture of her story was begun, though never finished, and they say it is somewhere in the house to this day, with its face to the wall.

Or, the uncle of my brother's wife was riding home on horseback, one mellow evening at sunset, when, in a green lane close to his own house, he saw a man standing before him, in the very centre of a narrow way. "Why does that man in the cloak stand there!" he thought "Does he want me to ride over him?" But the figure never moved. He felt a strange sensation at seeing it so still, but slackened his trot and rode forward When he was so close to it, as almost to touch it with his stirrup, his horse shied, and the figure glided up the bank, in a curious, unearthly manner—backward, and without seeming to use its feet—and was gone The uncle of my brother's wife, exclaiming, "Good Heavens! It's my cousin Harry, from Bombay!" put spurs to his horse, which was suddenly in a profuse sweat, and, wondering at such strange behaviour, dashed round to the front of his house. There, he saw the same figure, just passing in at the long French window of the drawing-room, opening on the ground. He threw his bridle to a servant, and hastened in after it His sister was sitting there, alone "Alice, where's my cousin Harry?" "Your cousin Harry, John?" "Yes From Bombay I met him in the lane just now, and saw him enter here, this instant." Not a creature had been seen by anyone; and in that hour and minute, as it afterwards appeared, this cousin died in India.

Or, it was a certain sensible old maiden lady, who died at ninety-nine, and retained her faculties to the last, who really did see the Orphan Boy; a story which has often been incorrectly told, but, of which the real truth is this—because it is, in fact, a story belonging to our family—and she was a connection of our family When she was about forty years of age, and still an uncommonly fine woman (her lover died young, which was the reason why she never married, though she had many offers), she went to stay at a place in Kent, which her brother, an Indian Merchant, had newly bought.

There was a story that this place had once been held in trust by the guardian of a young boy; who was himself the next heir, and who killed the young boy by harsh and cruel treatment. She knew nothing of that It has been said that there was a Cage in her bedroom in which the guardian used to put the boy. There was no such thing There was only a closet. She went to bed, made no alarm whatever in the night, and in the morning said composedly to her maid when she came in, "Who is the pretty forlorn-looking child who has been peeping out of that closet all night?" The maid replied by giving a loud scream, and instantly decamping. She was surprised; but she was a woman of remarkable strength of mind, and she dressed herself and went downstairs, and closeted herself with her brother "Now, Walter," she said, "I have been disturbed all night by a pretty, forlorn-looking boy, who has been constantly peeping out of that closet in my room, which I can't open. This is some trick" "I'm afraid not, Charlotte," said he, "for it is the legend of the house. It is the Orphan Boy. What did he do?" "He opened the door softly," said she, "and peeped out Sometimes he came a step or two into the room. Then, I called to him, to encourage him, and he shrunk, and shuddered, and crept in again, and shut the door "The closet has no communication, Charlotte," said her brother, "with any other part of the house, and it's nailed up." This was undeniably true, and it took two carpenters a whole forenoon to get it open for examination. Then, was she satisfied that she had seen the Orphan Boy. But, the terrible and wild part of the story is, that he was also seen by three of her brother's sons, in succession, who all died young. On the occasion of each child being taken ill, he came home in a heat, twelve hours before, and said, "Oh, Mamma," he had been playing under a particular oaktree, in a certain meadow, with a strange boy—a pretty forlorn-looking boy, who was very timid and made signs! From fatal experience, the parents came to know that this was the Orphan Boy, and that the course of that child whom he chose for his playmate was surely run.

Legion is the name of the German castles, where we sit up alone to wait for the Spectre—where we are shown into a room, made comparatively cheerful for our reception—where we glance round at the shadows, thrown on the blank galls by the crackling fire—where we feel very lonely when the village inn-keeper and his pretty daughter have retired, after laying down a fresh store of wood upon the hearth, and setting forth on the table such supper-cheer as a cold roast capon, bread, grapes, and a flask of old Rhine wine—where the reverberating doors close on their retreat, one after another, like so many peels of sullen thunder—and where, about the small hours of the night, we come into the knowledge of divers supernatural mysteries. Legion is the name of the haunted German students, in whose society we draw yet nearer to the fire—while the schoolboy in the corner opens his eyes wide and round, and flies off the footstool he has chosen for his seat, when the door accidentally blows open. Vast is the crop of such fruit, shining on our Christmas Tree; in blossom, almost at the very top; ripening all down the boughs!

Among the latter toys and fancies hanging there—as idle often and less pure—be the images once associated with the sweet old Waits, the softened music in the night, ever unalterable! Encircled by the social thoughts of Christmas-time, still let the benignant figure of my childhood stand unchanged! In every cheerful image and suggestion that the season brings, may the bright star that rested above the poor roof, be the star of all the Christian World! A moment's pause, O vanishing tree, of which the lower boughs are dark to me as yet, and let me look once more! I know there are blank spaces on thy branches, where eyes that I have loved have shone and smiled; from which they are departed. But, far above, I see the raiser of the dead girl, and the Widow's son; and God is good! If Age be hiding for me in the unseen portion of thy downward growth, O may I, with a grey head, turn a child's heart to that figure yet, and a child's trustfulness and confidence!

Now, the tree is decorated with bright merriment, and song, and dance, and cheerfulness. And they are welcome Innocent and welcome be they ever held, beneath the branches of the Christmas Tree, which cast no gloomy shadow! But, as it sinks into the ground, I hear a whisper go through the leaves "This, in commemoration of the law of love and kindness, mercy and compassion This, in remembrance of Me!"

Silent Night

JOSEPH MOHR

SILENT NIGHT, holy night,
All is calm, all is bright,
Round yon' Virgin mother and child,
Holy infant so tender and mild,
Sleep in heavenly peace,
Sleep in heavenly peace.

Silent night, holy night,
Shepherds quake at the sight;
Glory streams from heaven afar,
Heavenly hosts sing Alleluia.
Christ the Saviour is born!
Christ the Saviour is born!

Silent night, holy night,
Son of God, love's pure light;
Radiance beams from thy holy face,
With the dawn of redeeming grace,
Jesus, Lord at thy birth,
Jesus, Lord at thy birth.

How the Cat kept Christmas

(FROM *The New Year's Bargain* BY SUSAN COOLIDGE)

OFF THEY WENT, the magic stillness of the night broken only by the tinkling bells. First one chimney, then another; bag after bag full of toys and sweets; here a doll, there a diamond ring, here only a pair of warm stockings. Everybody had something, except in a few houses over whose roofs St Nicholas paused a moment with a look half sad, half angry, and left nothing. People lived there who knew him little, and loved him less.

Through the air—more towns—more villages. Now the sea was below them, the cold, moon-lit sea. Then again land came in sight—towers and steeples, halls and hamlets; and the work began again. A wild longing, seized the Cat. She begged the Saint to take her down one specially wide chimney on his shoulder. He did so. The nursery within looked strange and foreign; but the little sleeping face in bed was like Gretchen's and pussy felt at home. A whole bag full of presents was left here . . .

And then, hey! presto! they were off again to countless homes, to roofs so poor and low that only a Saint would have thought of visiting them, to stately palaces, to cellars and toll-gates and lonely attics; at last to a church, dim, and fragrant with ivy-leaves and twisted evergreen, where their errand was to feed a robin who had found shelter, and was sleeping on the topmost bough. How his beads of eyes sparkled as the Saint awoke him! and how eagerly he pecked the store of good red berries which were *his* Christmas present, though he had hung up no stocking and evidently expected nothing.

The Carol Singers

VIOLET BRADBY

THE CHILDREN of Wishford were resolved to go out carol singing this Christmas. They had often gone round singing before, but only by twos and threes, and without much practice. Last year, for instance, the two little Oakleys and Willy Barnes had wandered round the village piping out the three first verses of "While Shepherds Watched", without having taken the trouble even to learn the words by heart; and, in consequence, had been promptly chased away from most of the houses they had visited.

However, this year things were to be done very differently. As early as the beginning of November Dick Curtis had started the idea, and the other children had taken it up joyfully. At first they thought of excluding the girls, but later, more generously, they decided to ask them; for Dick suddenly remarked "Why shouldn't we?" and, as no one could think of a reason at the moment, they all said "Let's"; and thus it was settled.

The practices were held in a big hayloft over Mr. Curtis's cowshed, and the twelve carol singers crept stealthily thither across fields and along hedges. As a matter of fact, they drew attention to themselves much more by so doing than if they had walked there openly; but it added to the excitement of the thing.

Nicholas Moore was the youngest of them all. He was only seven, but he had begged so anxiously to be allowed to join, that the others had consented. He was small for his age, too, with very fair hair bleached nearly white by the sun, and round, enquiring, blue eyes.

One Saturday afternoon in the middle of December the carol singers had assembled as usual in the hayloft. They were seated on the piles of sweet-smelling hay, and the air was full of floating dust and hay seeds. Dick Curtis was standing in front of them, with a hazel twig in his hand to conduct with.

"Now," he began, "We'll start with 'Good King Wenceslaus'." There was always some hesitation about beginning, for Polly Green, the leader, was apt to start either very high, so that they found themselves squeaking up in the heights, or else very low, so that they had to grunt like bassoons. Today they started off quite safely, however, and with a great swing:

> "*Good* King Wenceslaus looked out
> *On* the Feast of Stephen".

After two verses Dick rapped with his hazel twig.
"*Someone* is singing like bass," he said firmly; "we

must begin again."

Everyone looked at everyone else in a reproachful manner, and then they began once more. After another verse Dick rapped again.

"It's no good," he said; "somebody is growling down low, and it spoils it all. Let's try 'Nowell, Nowell'; p'r'aps that'll go better."

Nicholas was sitting perched high up at the back of the group of children. He opened his mouth wide when he sang, with his round eyes fixed immovably on the young conductor, for he knew the words better than anybody; he never hesitated for a moment, and sang with his whole heart.

Dick let them sing all through the next carol; but then he shook his head and said: "It's no better; somebody's singing all wrong, and very loud too. whoever is it?"

There was a pause; then the children began whispering among themselves, and Dick caught one name repeated by everyone.

"Is it you, Nick?" he said reluctantly, for Nicholas was keener than anyone, and had never been absent from a practice.

Nicholas flushed crimson. "I dunno, Dick," he said, hanging his head.

"Try a verse alone," suggested one officious child.

"No," said Dick; "you stop singing for a bit, Nick, and we'll see if it makes any difference."

And it did. There was no longer any discordant

sound—the eleven voices rang out clear and true. Nicholas was the offender, there could be no doubt now.

"I thought it were he. I told Dick Curtis 'e couldn't keep the tune, and I were all right then," murmured the children among themselves.

Suddenly there was a shaking of the big haycock, and Nicholas came rolling and scrambling to the floor. He picked himself up, and stood covered with fragments of hay before Dick the conductor.

"It must have been me. I didn't know," he said in rather a quivering voice. "Jack Smith can sing fine, if you want another in—instead," and then he was gone.

It was Christmas Eve. Nicholas was sitting disconsolately on his little stool in the chimney corner, gazing at the fire, while his mother was busy in the back kitchen with preparations for the Christmas dinner.

"What's that? It sounds like carol singers. Run and see, Nicholas," she called presently.

Nicholas went to the window, pushed back the curtain a tiny bit, and peeped out. It was bright moonlight outside, and there, standing on the crisp white snow, was a group of dark figures. One of them carried a lantern, which cast a warm patch of orange light before it.

They were singing "The First Nowell", and when they had done that they sang "Now Carol We", and then one of the figures stepped up to the door and knocked. Nicholas rushed upstairs. Then his mother opened the door. She gave the children fourpence, praised their pretty singing, and wished them a Merry Christmas; then she called to ask Nicholas why he was such a silly as to run away. But Nicholas did not hear her. His head was thrust out of the casement window into the frosty air, and he was watching to see which way the carol singers went. Yes, it was just as he expected they had turned back towards the village. Then they were not going to old Betsy Morland's cottage.

Nicholas's mind was made up in a moment. He slipped downstairs, put on his cap and his scarlet comforter and his greatcoat which had been a jacket of his father's, and made him look like a tub on legs and while his mother was bending over her saucepans he opened the door and stepped out into the moonlight.

Betsy Morland was a very old widow who lived in the cottage down the lane all by herself. when Nicholas lifted the latch of her garden gate, he saw that there were no footmarks on the glistening snowy path, only near the door the snow was patterned by many birds' claws.

Nicholas stood near the little window, in which a light could be seen. He paused, took a deep breath, and then began. He chose his favourite carol, which was "Good King Wenceslaus", and as he sang his breath floated out in the cold air in little wreaths like smoke.

Old Betsy as darning a stocking, with her head bent close to the lamp, when the first notes of the carol fell on her ear. She raised her head and listened in astonishment. No one had ever thought it worth while to come and sing at her remote cottage before, and she could hardly believe her ears.

It was a funny little sound, certainly the tune moved along chiefly on one note, and there was more breath than tone but the words were plainly to be distinguished, even behind the closed lattice, and old Betsy thought it was beautiful.

Her first thought was: "And I haven't a pennypiece in the house, bless them!" for she imagined there were several children outside. Then she put down her stocking and hobbled across to the open door.

Nicholas sang louder than ever when he heard the latch go up, and as the door opened, and a shaft of light surrounded him, he stood shouting like a Robin on a twig with his mouth wide open:

"Fails my heart, I know not how;
I can go no longer".

"Why, goodness me, there's only one!" cried Betsy, and the next moment she had pulled Nicholas in out of the snowy garden, saying: "Now, sit ye down here by the fire and sing the dear old carols in the warm."

Nicholas glowed with satisfaction. He rid himself of his coat and cap, and, sitting in the big armchair with the patchwork cushion, sang gravely through every carol he knew, while old Betsy sat and listened. She thought it was heavenly, and she could have sat listening to his unmelodious singing with contentment for hours. She could hear every word, and she never knew that he made the tune sound the same for each carol; so what did it matter?

When he could remember no more, Betsy fetched a plate, and, putting a piece of cake and a rosy apple on it, offered it to Nicholas; and she told him how she used to go out "car'l singing" as a girl.

Nicholas munched his apple and listened, with his round eyes fixed on Betsy and his heart warm with pleasure.

"I think my carol singing was just as nice as theirs, after all," he thought to himself as he fell asleep that night to the sound of the Christmas bells.

THE TWELVE DAYS OF CHRISTMAS

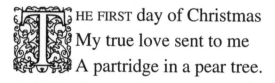HE FIRST day of Christmas
My true love sent to me
A partridge in a pear tree.

The second day of Christmas
My true love sent to me
Two turtle doves, and
A partridge in a pear tree.

The third day of Christmas
My true love sent to me
Three French hens,
Two turtle doves, and
A partridge in a pear tree.

The fourth day of Christmas
My true love sent to me
Four colly birds,
Three French hens,
Two turtle doves, and
A partridge in a pear tree.

The fifth day of Christmas
My true love sent to me
Five gold rings,
Four colly birds,
Three French hens,
Two turtle doves, and
A partridge in a pear tree.

The sixth day of Christmas
My true love sent to me
Six geese a-laying,
Five gold rings,
Four colly birds,
Three French hens,
Two turtle doves, and
A partridge in a pear tree.

The seventh day of Christmas
My true love sent to me
Seven swans a-swimming,
Six geese a-laying,
Five gold rings,
Four colly birds,
Three French hens,
Two turtle doves, and
A partridge in a pear tree.

The eighth day of Christmas
My true love sent to me
Eight maids a-milking,
Seven swans a-swimming,
Six geese a-laying,
Five gold rings,
Four colly birds,
Three French hens,
Two turtle doves, and
A partridge in a pear tree.

The ninth day of Christmas
My true love sent to me
Nine drummers drumming,
Eight maids a-milking,
Seven swans a-swimming,
Six geese a-laying,
Five gold rings,
Four colly birds,
Three French hens,
Two turtle doves, and
A partridge in a pear tree.

The tenth day of Christmas
My true love sent to me
Ten pipers piping,
Nine drummers drumming,
Eight maids a-milking,
Seven swans a-swimming,
Six geese a-laying,
Five gold rings,
Four colly birds,
Three French hens,
Two turtle doves, and
A partridge in a pear tree.

The eleventh day of Christmas
My true love sent to me
Eleven ladies dancing,
Ten pipers piping,
Nine drummers drumming,
Eight maids a-milking,
Seven swans a-swimming,
Six geese a-laying,
Five gold rings,
Four colly birds,
Three French hens,
Two turtle doves, and
A partridge in a pear tree.

The twelfth day of Christmas
My true love sent to me
Twelve lords a-leaping,
Eleven ladies dancing,
Ten pipers piping,
Nine drummers drumming,
Eight maids a-milking,
Seven swans a-swimming,
Six geese a-laying,
Five gold rings,
Four colly birds,
Three French hens,
Two turtle doves, and
A partridge in a pear tree.

Christmas is Coming

CHRISTMAS IS COMING

CHRISTMAS is coming
    The goose is getting fat,
Please put a penny
    In the old man's hat.
If you haven't got a penny
    A ha'penny will do,
If you haven't got a ha'penny,
    God bless you.

The Snow Queen

HANS CHRISTIAN ANDERSEN

The Mirror and its Fragments

THERE WAS once a magician, a wicked magician, a most wicked magician. Great was his delight at having constructed a mirror possessing this peculiarity, that everything good and beautiful,when reflected in it, shrank up almost to nothing, whilst those things that were ugly and useless were magnified and made to appear ten times worse than before. The loveliest landscapes reflected in this mirror looked like boiled spinach; and the handsomest persons appeared odious, or as if standing upon their heads, their features being so distorted that their friends could never have recognised them. Moreover, if one of them had a freckle, he might be sure that it would seem to spread over the nose and mouth; and if a good or pious thought glanced across his mind, a wrinkle was seen in the mirror. All this the magician thought highly entertaining, and he chuckled with delight at his own clever invention. Those who frequented the school of magic where he taught, spread abroad the fame of this wonderful mirror, and declared that by its means the world and its inhabitants might be seen now for the first time as they really were. They carried the mirror from place to place, till at last there was no country nor person that had not been misrepresented in it. Its admirers now must needs fly up to the sky with it, to see if they could not carry on their sport even there. But the higher they flew the more wrinkled did the mirror become; they could scarcely hold it together. They flew on and on, higher and higher, till at last the mirror trembled so fearfully that it escaped from their hands and fell to the earth, breaking into millions, billions, and trillions of pieces. And then it caused far greater unhappiness than before, for fragments of it scarcely as large as a grain of sand flew about in the air, and sometimes got into people's eyes, causing them to view everything the wrong way, or to have eyes only for what was perverted and corrupt; each little fragment having retained the peculiar properties of the entire mirror. Some people were so unfortunate as to receive a little splinter into their hearts— that was terrible! The heart became cold and hard, like a lump of ice. Some pieces were large enough to be used as window-panes, but it was of no use to look at one's friends through such panes as those. Other fragments were made into spectacles, and then what trouble people had with setting and re-setting them!

The wicked magician was greatly amused with all this, and he laughed till his sides ached.

There are still some little splinters of this mischievous mirror flying about in the air. We shall hear more about them very soon.

A LTTLE BOY AND A LITTLE GIRL

In a large town where there are so many houses and in-habitants that there is not room enough for all the people to possess a little garden of their own, and therefore many are obliged to content themselves with keeping a few plants in pots, there dwelt two poor children, whose gar-den was somewhat larger than a flower-pot. They were not brother and sister, but they loved each other as much as if they had been, and their parents lived in two attics which were exactly opposite each other. The roof of one house nearly joined the other, the gutter ran along be-tween, and there was in each roof a little window, so that you could stride across the gutter from one window to the other. The parents of each child had a large wooden box in which grew herbs for kitchen use, and they had placed these boxes upon the gutter, so near that they almost touched each other. A beautiful little rosetree grew in each box; scarlet-runners entwined their long shoots over the windows, and, uniting with the branches of the rose trees, formed a flowery arch across the street. The boxes were very high, and the children knew that they might not climb over them, but they often obtained leave to sit on their little stools, under the rose trees, and thus they passed many a delightful hour.

But when winter came there was an end to these pleasures. The windows were often quite frozen over, and then they heated halfpence on the stove, held the warm copper against the frozen pane, and thus made a little round peep-hole through which they could see each other.

The little boy was called Kay; the little girl's name was Gerda. In summer they could get out of the window and jump over to each other; but in winter there were stairs to run down and stairs to run up, and sometimes the wind roared and the snow fell without doors.

"Those are the white bees swarming there!" said the old grandmother.

"Have they a Queen bee?" asked the little boy, for he knew that the real bees have one.

"They have," said the grandmother. "She flies yonder where they swarm so thickly; she is the largest of them, and never remains upon the earth, but flies up again into the black cloud. Sometimes on a winter's night she flies through the streets of the town, and breathes with her frosty breath upon the windows, and then they are covered with strange and beautiful forms like trees and flowers."

"Yes, I have seen them!" said both the children—they knew that this was true.

"Can the Snow Queen come in here?" asked the little girl.

"If she do come in," said the boy, "I will put her on the

warm stove, and then she will melt."

And the grandmother stroked his hair and told him stories.

That same evening, after little Kay had gone home and was half undressed he crept upon the chair by the window and peeped through the little round hole. Just then a few snowflakes fell outside, and one, the largest of them, remained lying on the edge of one of the flower-pots. The snowflake appeared larger and larger, and at last took the form of a lady dressed in the finest white crape, her attire being composed of millions of star-like particles. She was exquisitely fair and delicate, but entirely of ice, glittering, dazzling ice; her eyes gleamed like two bright stars, but there was no rest or repose in them. She nodded at the window, and beckoned with her hand. The little boy was frightened and jumped down from the chair; he then fancied he saw a large bird fly past the window.

There was a clear frost next day, and soon afterwards came spring,—the trees and flowers budded, the swallows built their nests, the windows were opened, and the little children sat once more in their little garden upon the gutter that ran along the roofs of the houses.

The roses blossomed beautifully that summer, and the little girl had learned a hymn in which there was something about roses; it reminded her of her own. So she sang it to the little boy, and he sang it with her.

Our roses bloom and fade away,
Our Infant Lord abides alway;
May we be blessed His face to see,
And ever little children be!

And the little ones held each other by the hand, kissed the roses, and looked up into the blue sky, talking away all the time. What glorious summer days were those! how delightful it was to sit under those rose-trees, which seemed as if they never intended to leave off blossoming!

One day Kay and Gerda were sitting looking at their picture book full of birds and animals, when suddenly Kay exclaimed, "Oh, dear! what was that shooting pain in my heart! and oh, something has got into my eye!"

The little girl turned and looked at him. He winked his eyes; no, there was nothing to be seen.

"I believe it is gone," said he; but gone it was not. It was one of those glass splinters from the Magic Mirror, the wicked glass which made everything great and good reflected in it appear little and hateful, and which magnified everything ugly and mean. Poor Kay had also received a splinter in his heart; it would now become hard and cold like a lump of ice. He felt the pain no longer, but the splinter was there.

"Why do you cry?" asked he. "You look so ugly when you cry! There is nothing the matter with me. Fie!" he exclaimed again, "this rose has an insect in it. And just look at this! After all, they are ugly roses, and it is an ugly box they grow in." Then he kicked the box, and tore off the roses.

"Oh, Kay, what are you doing?" cried the little girl. But when he saw how it grieved her, he tore off another rose, and jumped down through his own window, away from his once dear little Gerda.

Ever afterwards, when she brought forward the picture-book, he called it a baby's book, and when her grand-mother told stories, he interrupted her with a "but," and sometimes, whenever he could manage it, he would get behind her, put on her spectacles, and speak just as she did; he did this in a very droll manner, and so people laughed at him. Very soon he could mimic everybody in the street. All that was singular and awkward about them Kay could imitate, and his neighbours said, "what a re-markable head that boy has!" But no, it was the glass splinter which had fallen into his eye, the glass splinter which had pierced into his heart—it was these which made him regardless whose feelings he wounded, and even made him tease the little Gerda.

One day Kay came in with thick gloves on his hands and his sledge slung across his back. He called out to Gerda, "I have got leave to drive on the great square where the other boys play!" and away he went.

The boldest boys in the square used to fasten their sledges firmly to the waggons of the country people, and thus drive a good way along with them; this they thought particularly pleasant. Whilst they were in the midst of their play, a large sledge painted white passed by; in it sat a person wrapped in a rough white fur, and wearing a rough white cap. When the sledge had driven twice round the square, Kay bound to it his little sledge, and was carried on with it. On they went, faster and faster, into the next street. The person who drove the large sledge turned round and nodded kindly to Kay, just as if they had been old acquaintances, and every time Kay was going to loose his little sledge, turned and nodded again, as if to signify that he must stay. So Kay sat still, and they passed through the gates of the town. Then the snow began to fall so thickly that the little boy could not see his own hand, but he was still carried on. He tried hastily to unloose the cords and free himself from the large sledge, but it was of no use; his little carriage could not be unfastened, and glided on swift as the wind. Then he cried out as loud as he could, but no one heard him. The snow fell and the sledge flew; every now and then it made a spring as if driving over hedges and ditches. He was very much frightened; he could have repeated "Our Father," but he could remember nothing but the multiplication table.

The snow-flakes seemed larger and larger, till at last they looked like great white fowls. All at once they fell aside, the large sledge stopped, and the person who drove it rose from the seat. Kay saw that the cap and coat were entirely of snowy, that it was a lady, tall and slender, and dazzlingly white—it was the Snow Queen!

"We have driven fast!" said she, "but no one likes to be

frozen. Creep under my bear-skin." And she seated him in the sledge by her side, and spread her cloak; around him—he felt as if he were sinking into a drift of snow.

"Are you still cold?" asked she, and then she kissed his brow. Oh! her kiss was colder than ice. It went to his heart, although that was half frozen already; he thought he should die. It was, however, only for a moment; directly afterwards he was quite well, and no longer felt the intense cold around.

"My sledge! Do not forget my sledge!" He thought first of that. It was fastened to one of the white fowls, which flew behind with it on his back. The Snow Queen kissed Kay again, and he entirely forgot little Gerda, her grandmother, and all at home.

"Now you must have no more kisses!" said she, "else I should kiss thee to death."

Kay looked at her. She was very beautiful; a more intelligent, more lovely countenance, he could not imagine. She no longer appeared to him ice, cold ice, as at the time when she sat outside the window and beckoned to him; in his eyes she was perfect; he felt no fear. He told her how well he could reckon in his head, even fractions; that he knew the number of square miles of every country, and the number of the inhabitants in different towns. She smiled, and then it occurred to him that, after all, he did not yet know so very much. He looked up into the wide, wide space, and she flew with him high up into the black cloud while the storm was raging; it seemed now to

Kay to be singing songs of olden time.

They flew over woods and over lakes, over sea and over land. Beneath them the cold wind whistled, the wolves howled, the snow glittered, and the black crow flew cawing over the plain, whilst above them shone the moon, clear and tranquil.

Thus did Kay spend the long, long winter night; all day he slept at the feet of the Snow Queen.

THE ENCHANTED FLOWER GARDEN

But how fared it with little Gerda when Kay never returned? Where could he be? No one knew. The boys said they had seen him fasten his sledge to another larger and very handsome one which had driven into the street, and thence through the gates of the town. No one knew where he was, and many were the tears that were shed. Little Gerda wept much and long, for the boys said he must have been drowned in the river that flowed not far from the town. Oh, how long and dismal the winter days were now! At last came the spring with its warm sunshine.

"Alas, Kay is dead and gone," said little Gerda.

"That I do not believe," said the sunshine.

"He is dead and gone," said she to the swallows.

"That we do not believe," returned they, and at last little Gerda herself did not believe it.

"I will put on my new red shoes," said she one morning, "those which Kay has never seen, and then I will go down to the river and ask after him."

It was quite early. She kissed her old grandmother, who was still sleeping, put on her red shoes, and went alone through the gates of the town towards the river.

"Is it true," said she, "that you have taken my little playfellow away? I will give you my red shoes if you will restore him to me!"

And the wavelets of the river flowed towards her in a manner which she fancied was unusual; she fancied that they intended to acceppt her offer, so she took off her red shoes—though she prized them more than anything else she possesed—and threw them into the stream; but the little waves bore them back to her, as though they would not take from her what she most prized, as they had not got little Kay. However, she thought she had not thrown the shoes far enough, so she stepped into a little boat which lay among the reeds by the shore, and, standing at the farthest end of it, threw them thence into the water. The boat was not fastened, and her movements in it caused it to glide away from the shore. She saw this, and hastened to get out, but by the time she reached the other end of the boat, it was more than a yard from the land; she could not escape, and the boat glided on.

Little Gerda was much frightened and began to cry, but no one besides the sparrows heard her, and they could not carry her back to the land; however, they flew along the banks, and sang, as if to comfort her, "Here we are, here we are!" The boat followed the stream.

"Perhaps the river may bear me to my dear Kay," thought Gerda, and then she became more cheerful, and amused herself for hours with looking at the lovely country around her. At last she glided past a large cherry garden, wherein stood a little cottage with thatched roof and curious red and blue windows. Two wooden soldiers stood at the door, who presented arms when they saw the little vessel approach.

Gerda called to them, thinking that they were alive, but they, naturally enough, made no answer. She came close up to them, for the stream drifted the boat to the land.

Gerda called still louder, whereupon an old lady came out of the house, supporting herself on a crutch. She wore a large hat, with most beautiful flowers painted on it.

"Poor little child!" said the old woman. "The mighty flowing river has indeed borne you a long, long way." And she walked right into the water, seized the boat with her crutch, drew it to land, and took out the little girl.

Gerda was glad to be on dry land again, although she was a little afraid of the strange old lady.

"Come and tell me who you are, and how you came hither," said she.

Gerda told her all, and the old lady shook her head, and said, "Hem! hem!" And when Gerda asked if she had seen little Kay, the lady said that he had not arrived there yet, but that he would be sure to come soon, and that in the meantime Gerda must not be sad; that she might stay with her, might eat her cherries, and look at her flowers, which were prettier than any picture book, and could each tell her a story.

She then took Gerda by the hand; they went together into the cottage, and the old lady shut the door. The windows were very high and their panes of different coloured glass, red, blue, and yellow, so that when the bright daylight streamed through them, various and beautiful were the hues reflected upon the room. Upon a table in the centre was placed a plate of very fine cherries, and of these Gerda was allowed to eat as many as she liked. And whilst she was eating them, the old dame combed her hair with a golden comb, and the bright flaxen ringlets fell on each side of her pretty, gentle face, which looked as round and as fresh as a rose.

"I have long wished for such a dear little girl," said the old lady. "We shall see if we cannot live very happily together." And, as she combed little Gerda's hair, the child thought less and less of Kay, for the old lady was an enchantress. She did not, however, practise magic for the sake of mischief, but merely for her own amusement. And now she wished very much to keep little Gerda, to live with her; so, fearing that if Gerda saw her roses she would be reminded of her own flowers and of little Kay, and that then she might run away, she went out into the garden, and extended her crutch over all her rose-bushes, upon which, although they were full of leaves and blossoms, they immediately sank into the black earth.

Then she led Gerda into this flower-garden. Flowers of

all seasons and all climes grew there in fulness of beauty—certainly no picture-book could be compared with it. Gerda bounded with delight, and played among the flowers till the sun set behind the tall cherry-trees. Then a pretty little bed, with crimson silk cushions, stuffed with blue violet leaves, was prepared for her, and there she slept so sweetly and had such dreams as a queen might have on her bridal eve.

The next day she again played among the flowers in the warm sunshine, and many more days she spent in the same manner. Gerda knew every flower in the garden, but, numerous as they were, it seemed to her that one was wanting, she could not tell which. She was sitting one day, looking at her hostess's hat, which had flowers painted on it, and, behold, the loveliest among them was a rose! The old lady had entirely forgotten the painted rose on her hat when she made the real roses disappear from her garden and sink into the ground.

"What," cried Gerda, "are there no roses in the garden?" She ran from one bed to another, sought and sought again, but no rose was to be found. She sat down and wept, and it so chanced that her tears fell on a spot where a rose-tree had formerly stood, and as soon as her warm tears had moistened the earth, the bush shot up anew, as fresh and as blooming as it was before it had sunk into the ground; and Gerda threw her arms around it, kissed the blossoms, and immediately recalled to memory the beautiful roses at home, and her little playfellow Kay. "Oh, how could I stay here so long!" she exclaimed. "I left my home to seek for Kay. Do you know where he is?" she asked of the roses. "Is he dead?"

"Dead he is not," said the roses. "We have been down in the earth; the dead are there, but not Kay."

"I thank you," said little Gerda, and she went to the other flowers, and asked, "Know you not where little Kay is?"

But every flower stood in the sunshine dreaming its own little tale. They related their stories to Gerda, but none of them knew anything of Kay.

So away she ran to the end of the garden.

The gate was closed, but she pressed upon the rusty lock till it broke. The gate sprang open, and little Gerda, with bare feet, ran out into the wide world. Three times she looked back; there was no one following her. She ran till she could run no longer, and then sat down to rest upon a large stone. Casting a glance around, she saw that the summer was past, that it was now late in the autumn. She had not remarked this in the enchanted garden, where there were sunshine and flowers all the year round.

"How long I must have stayed there!" said little Gerda. "So it is now autumn! Well, then, there is no time to lose!" And she rose to pursue her way.

Oh, how sore and weary were her little feet! And all around looked so cold and barren. The long willow-leaves had already turned yellow, and the dew trickled down from them like water. The leaves fell off the trees,

The Snow Queen

one by one; the sloe alone bore fruit, and its berries were sharp and bitter! Cold, and grey, and sad seemed the world to her that day.

THE PRINCE AND THE PRINCESS

Gerda was again obliged to stop and take rest. Suddenly a large raven hopped upon the snow in front of her, saying, "Caw!—Caw!—Good-day!—Good-day!" He sat for some time or the withered branch of a tree just opposite, eyeing the little maiden, and wagging his head, and he now came forward to make acquaintance and to ask her whither she was going all alone. Gerda told the raven the history of her life and fortunes.

And the raven nodded his head, half doubtfully, and said, "That is possible—possible."

"Do you think so?" exclaimed the little girl, and she kissed the raven so vehemently that it is a wonder she did not squeeze him to death.

"More moderately!—moderately!" said the raven. "I think I know. I think it may be little Kay; but he has certainly forsaken you for the princess."

"Does he dwell with a princess?" asked Greda.

"Listen to me," said the raven; "but it is so difficult to speak your language! Do you understand Ravenish? If so, I can tell you much better."

"No! I have never learned Ravenish," said Greda; "but my grandmother knew it. Oh, how I wish I had learned it!"

"Never mind," said the raven, "I will relate my story in the best manner I can"; and he told all he knew.

"In the kingdom wherein we are now sitting, there dwells a most uncommonly clever princess. Immediately after she ascended the throne she began to sing a new song, the burden of which was this, 'Why should I not marry me?' 'There is some sense in this song!' said she, and she determined she would marry, but declared that the man whom she would choose must be able to answer sensibly whenever people spoke to him, and must be good for something else besides merely looking grand and stately. Believe me," continued the raven, "every word I say is true, for I have a tame beloved who hops at pleasure about the palace, and she has told me all this.

"Proclamations, adorned with borders of hearts, were immediately issued, wherein it was set forth that every well-favoured youth was free to go to the palace, and that whoever should converse with the princess so as to show that he felt himself at home would be the one the princess would choose for her husband.

"The people all crowded to the palace; but it was all of no use. The young men could speak well enough while they were outside the palace gates but when they entered, and saw the royal guard in silver uniform, and the lackeys on the staircase in gold, and the spacious saloon, all lighted up, they were quite confounded. They stood before the throne where the princess sat, and when she spoke to them they could only repeat the last word she had uttered. It was just as though they had been struck dumb the moment they entered the palace, for as soon as they got out they could talk fast enough. There was a regular procession constantly moving from the gates of the town to the gates of the palace."

"But Kay, little Kay, when did he come?" asked Gerda. "Was he among the crowd?"

"Presently, presently; we have just come to him. On the third day arrived a youth with neither horse nor carriage. Gaily he marched up to the palace. His eyes sparkled like yours; he had long beautiful hair, but was very meanly clad."

"That was Kay!" exclaimed Gerda. "Oh then I have found him!" and she clapped her hands with delight.

"He carried a knapsack on his back," said the raven.

"No, not a knapsack," said Gerda, "a sledge, for he had a sledge with him when he left home."

"It is possible," rejoined the raven, "I did not look very closely; but this I heard from my beloved, that when he entered the palace gates and saw the royal guard in silver, and the lackeys in gold upon the staircase, he did not seem in the least confused, but nodded pleasantly and said to them, 'It must be very tedious standing out here, I prefer going in.' The halls glistened with light, cabinet councillors and excellencies were walking about barefooted and carrying golden keys—it was just a place to make a man solemn and silent—and the youth's boots creaked horribly, yet he was not at all afraid."

"That most certainly was Kay!" said Gerda; "I know he had new boots; I have heard them creak in my grandmother's room."

"Indeed they did creak," said the raven, "but merrily went he up to the princess, who was sitting upon a pearl as large as a spinning-wheel, whilst all the ladies of the court, with the maids of honour and their handmaidens, ranged in order, stood on one side, and all the gentlemen in waiting, with their gentlemen, and their gentlemen's gentlemen, who also kept pages, stood ranged in order on the other side, and the nearer they were to the door the prouder they looked.

"The young man spoke as well as I speak when I converse in Ravenish. He was handsome and lively. He did not come to woo her, he said, he had only come to hear the wisdom of the princess. And he liked her much, and she liked him in return."

"Yes, to be sure, that was Kay," said Gerda. "He was so clever, he could reckon in his head, even fractions! Oh, will you not take me into the palace?"

"Ah! that is easily said," replied the raven, "but how is it to be done? I will talk it over with my tame beloved; she will advise us what to do, for I must tell you that such a little girl as you are will never gain permission to enter publicly."

"Yes, I shall!" cried Gerda. "When Kay knows that I am here, he will immediately come out and fetch me."

'Wait for me at the trellis yonder," said the raven. He

wagged his head and away he flew.

The raven did not return till late in the evening. "Caw, caw," said he. "My tame beloved greets you kindly, and sends you a piece of bread which she took from the kitchen; there is plenty of bread there, and you must certainly be hungry. As you have bare feet, the royal guard in silver uniform, and the lackeys in gold, would never permit you to enter the palace; but do not weep you shall go there. My beloved knows a little back staircase leading to the sleeping apartments, and she knows also where to find the key."

So they went into the garden, and down the grand avenue, and, when the lights in the palace one by one had all been extinguished, the raven took Gerda to a back-door which stood half open. Oh, how Gerda's heart beat with fear and expectation! It was just as though she was about to do something wrong, although she only wanted to know whether Kay was really there. She would see if his smile were the same as it used to be when they sat together under the rose-trees. He would be so glad to see her, to hear how far she had come for his sake, how all at home mourned his absence. Her heart trembled with fear and joy.

They went up the staircase. A small lamp placed on a cabinet gate a glimmering light; on the floor stood the tame raven, who first turned her head on all sides, and then looked at Gerda, who made her curtsey, as her grandmother had taught her.

"My betrothed has told me much about you, my good young maiden," said the tame raven; "your adventures, too, are extremely interesting! If you will take the lamp, I will show you the way. We are going straight on; we shall not meet any one now"

They now entered the first saloon; its walls were covered with rose-coloured satin, embroidered with gold flowers. The Dreams rustled past them, but with such rapidity that Gerda could not see them. The apartments through which they passed tied with each other in splendour, and at last they reached the sleeping-hall. In the centre of this room stood a pillar of gold resembling the stem of a large palm-tree whose leaves of glass, costly glass, formed the ceiling, and depending from the tree, hung near the door, on thick golden stalls, were two beds in the form of likes. One was white, and in it reposed the princess. The other was red, and in it Gerda sought her play fellow, Kay. She bent aside one of the red leaves and saw a brown neck. Oh, it must be Kay! She called him by his name aloud, and held the lamp close to him. The Dreams rushed by—he awoke, turned his head, and behold! it was not Kay.

The princess looked out from the white lily petals, and aslied what was the matter. Then little Gerda wept, and told her whole story, and what the ravens had done for her. "Poor child!" said the prince and princess; and they praised the ravens, and said they were not at all angry with them. Such liberties must never be taken again in their palace, but this time they should be rewarded.

"Would you like to fly away free to the woods?" asked the princess, addressing the ravens, "or to have the appointment secured to you as Court-Ravens with the perquisites belonging to the kitchen, such as crumbs and leavings?"

And both the ravens bowed low and chose the appointment at Court, for they thought of old age, and said it would be so comfortable to be well provided for in their declining years. Then the prince rose and made Gerda sleep in his bed.

The next day she was dressed from head to foot in silk and velvet. She was invited to stay at the palace and enjoy all sorts of diversions, but she begged only for a little carriage and a horse, and a pair of little boots. All she desired was to go again into the wide world to seek Kay.

They gave her the boots and a muff besides. And as soon as she was ready there drove up to the door a new carriage of pure gold with the arms of the prince and princess glittering upon it like a star, the coachman, the footman, and outriders, all wearing gold crowns. The prince and princess themselves helped her into the carriage and wished her success. The wood-raven, who was now married, accompanied her the first three miles. The carriage was well provided with sugar-plums, fruit, and gingerbread nuts.

"Farewell! farewell!" cried the prince and princess. Little Gerda wept, and the raven wept out of sympathy. Then he flew up to the branch of a tree and flapped his black wings at the carriage till it was out of sight.

They drove through the dark, dark forest; the carriage shone like a torch. Unfortunately its brightness attracted the eyes of the robbers who dwelt in the forest-shades.

"That is gold! gold!" cried they. Forward they rushed, seized the horses, stabbed the outriders, coachman, and footman to death, and dragged little Gerda out of the carriage.

"She is plump, she is pretty, she has been fed on nutkernels," said the old robber-wife, who had a long, bristly beard, and eyebrows hanging like bushes over her eyes. "She is like a little fat lamb, and how smartly she is dressed!" And she drew out her bright dagger, glittering most terribly.

"Oh, oh!" cried the woman, for at the very moment she had lifted her dagger to stab Gerda, her own wild and wilful daughter jumped upon her back and bit her ear violently. "You naughty child!" said the mother.

"She shall play with me," said the little robber- maiden. "She shall give me her muff and her pretty frock, and sleep with me in my bed!" And then she bit her mother again, till the robber-wife sprang up and shrieked with pain? whilst the robbers all laughed, saying, "Look at her playing with her young one!"

So spoiled and wayward was the little robber-maiden that she always had her own way, and she and Gerda sat together in the carriage, and drove farther and farther into the wood. The little robber-maiden was about as tall as Gerda, but much stronger; she had broad shoulders, and a very dark skin; her eyes were quite black, and had an expression almost melancholy. She put her arm round Gerda's waist, and said, "She shall not kill you so long as I love you! Are you not a princess?"

"No!" said Gerda; and then she told her all that had happened to her, and how much she loved little Kay.

The robber-maiden looked earnestly in her face, shook her head, and said, "She shall not kill you even if I do quarrel with you; then, indeed, I would rather do it myself!" And she dried Gerda's tears, and put both her hands into the pretty muff that was so soft and warm.

The carriage at last stopped in the middle of the courtvard of the robbers' castle. This castle was half ruined; crows and ravens flew out of the openings, and some fearfully large bulldogs, looking as if they could devour a man in a moment, jumped round the carriage; they did not bark, for that was forbidden.

The maidens entered a large, smoky hall, where a tremendous fire was blazing on the stone floor. A large cauldron full of soup was boiling over the fire, whilst hares and rabbits were roasting on the spit.

"You shall sleep with me and my little pets tonight," said the robber-maiden. Then they had some food, and afterwards went to the corner where lay straw and a piece of carpet. Nearly a hundred pigeons were perched on staves and laths around them; they seemed to be asleep, but were startled when the little maidens approached.

"These all belong to me," said Gerda's companion, and seizing hold of one of the nearest, she held the poor bird by the feet and swung it. "Miss it," said she, flapping it into Gerda's face. "The rabble from the wood sit up there," continued she, pointing to a number of laths fastened across a hole in the wall; "those are wood-pigeons, they would fly away if I did not keep them shut up. And here is my old favourite!" She pulled forward by the horn a reindeer who wore a bright copper ring round his neck, by which he was fastened to a large stone. "We are obliged to chain him up, or he would run away from us. Every evening I tickle his neck uith my sharp dagger; it makes him fear me so much!" And the robber-maiden drew out a long dagger from a gap in the wall and passed it over the reindeer's throat. The poor animal struggled and kicked, but the girl laughed, and then she pulled Gerda into bed with her.

"Will you keep the dagger in your hand whilst you sleep?" asked Gerda, looking timidly at the dangerous plaything

"I always sleep with my dagger by my side," replied the little robber-maiden. "One never knows what may happen. But now tell me all over again what you told me before about Kay, and the reason of your coming into the wide world all by yourself."

Gerda again related her history, and the wood-pigeons imprisoned above listened, but the others were fast asleep. The little robber-maiden threw one arm round Gerda's neck, and holding the dagger with the other, was also soon asleep. But Gerda could not close her eyes throughout the night—she knew not what would become of her, whether she would even be suffered to live. The robbers sat round the fire drinking and singing. Oh, it was a dreadful night for the poor little girl!

Then spoke the wood-pigeons, "Coo, coo, coo we have seen little Kay. A white fowl carried his sledge; he himself was in the Snow Queen's chariot, which passed through the wood whilst we sat in our nest. She breathed upon us young ones as she passed, and all died of her breath excepting us two,—coo, coo, coo!"

"What are you saying?" cried Gerda. "Where was the Snow Queen going? Do you know anything about it?"

"She travelled most likely to Lapland, where ice and snow abide all the year round. Ask the reindeer bound to the rope there."

"Yes, ice and snow are there all through the year; it is a glorious land!" said the reindeer. "There, free and happy, one can roam through the wide sparkling valleys! There the Snow Queen has her summer-tent; her strong castle is very far off, near the North Pole, on the island called Spitzbergen."

"O Kay, dear Kay!" sighed Gerda.

When morning came Gerda repeated to her what the woodpigeons had said, and the little robber-maiden looked grave for a moment, then nodded her head. "Do you know where Lapland is?" asked she of the reindeer.

"Who should know but I!" returned the animal, his eyes kindling. "There was I born and bred; there, how often have I bounded over the wild, icy plains!"

"Listen to me!" said the robber-maiden to Gerda. "You see all our men are gone, my mother is still here and will remain, but towards noon she will drink a little out of the great flask, and after that she will sleep—then I will do something for you!"

When her mother was fast asleep, the robber-maiden went up to the reindeer and said, "I should have great pleasure in stroking you a few more times with my sharp dagger, for then you look so droll; but never mind, I will unloose your chain and help you to escape, on condition that you run as fast as you can to Lapland, and take this little girl to the castle of the Snow Queen, where her playfellow is. You must have heard her story, for she speaks loud enough, and you know well how to listen.

The reindeer bounded with joy, and the robber-maiden lifted Gerda on his back, taking the precaution to bind her on firmly, as well as to give her a little cushion on which to sit. "And here," said she, "are your fur boots. You will need them in that cold country. The muff I must keep myself; it is too pretty to part with. But you shall not be frozen. Here are my mother's huge gloves; they reach up to the elbow. Put them on—now your hands look as clumsy as my old mother's"

Gerda shed tears of joy.

"I cannot bear to see you crying!" said the little robbermaiden. "You ought to look glad. See, here are two loaves and a piece of bacon for you, that you may not be hungry on the way." She fastened this provender also on the reindeer's back, opened the door, called away the great dogs, and then, cutting asunder with her dagger the rope which bound the reindeer, shouted to him, "Now then, run! but take good care of the little girl."

Gerda stretched out her hands to the robber-maiden and bade her farewell, and the reindeer bounded through the forest, over stock and stone, over desert and heath, over meadow and moor. The wolves howled and the ravens shrieked. "Isch! Isch!" a red light flashed—one might have fancied the sky was sneezing.

"Those are my dear old Northern Lights!" said the reindeer. "Look at them, how beautiful they are!" And he ran faster than ever. Night and day he ran—the loaves were eaten, so was the bacon—at last they were in Lapland.

THE LAPLAND WOMAN AND THE FINLAND WOMAN

They stopped at a little hut. A wretched hut it was; the roof very nearly touched the ground, and the door was so low that whoever wished to go either in or out was obliged to crawl upon hands and knees. No one was at home except an old Lapland woman who was busy boiling fish over a lamp. The reindeer related to her Gerda's whole history—not, however, till after he had made her acquainted with his own, which appeared to him of much more importance. Poor Gerda, meanwhile, was so over-powered by the cold that she could not speak.

"Ah, poor thing!" said the Lapland woman, "you have still a long way before you! You have a hundred miles to run before you can arrive in Finland: the Snow Queen dwells there, and burns blue lights every evening. I will write for you a few words on a piece of dried stock-fish—paper I have none—and you may take it with you to the wise Finland woman who lives there; she will advise you better than I can."

So when Gerda had well warmed herself and taken some food, the Lapland woman wrote a few words on a dried stock-fish, bade Gerda take care of it, and bound her once more firmly on the reindeer's back.

Onwards they sped; the wondrous Northern Lights, now of the loveliest, brightest blue colour, shone all through the night, and amidst these splendid illumina-tions they arrived in Finland, and knocked at the chimney of the wise woman, for door to her house she had none.

Hot, very hot was it within—so much so that the wise woman wore scarcely any clothing. She was low in stat-ure and very dirty. She immediately loosened little Gerda's dress, took off her fur boots and thick gloves, laid a piece of ice on the reindeer's head, and then read what was written on the stock-fish. She read it three times. Af-ter the third reading she knew it by heart, so she threw the fish into the porridge-pot, for it might make a very excellent supper, and she never wasted anything.

The reindeer then repeated his own story, and when that was finished he told of little Gerda's adventures, and the wise woman twinkled her wise eyes but spoke not a word.

"Will you not mix for this little maiden that wonderful draught which will give her the strength of twelve men, and thus enable her to overcome the Snow Queen?" said the reindeer.

"The strength of twelve men!" repeated the wise woman, "that would be of much use to be sure!" And she walked away, drew forth a large parchment roll from a shelf, and began to read. She read so intently that the perspiration ran down her forehead.

At last the wise woman's eyes began to twinkle again, and she drew the reindeer into a corner, and putting a fresh piece of ice upon his head, whispered thus: "Little Kay is still with the Snow Queen, in whose abode everything is according to his taste, and therefore he believes it to be the best place in the world. But that is because he has a glass splinter in his heart and a glass splinter in his eye. Until he has got rid of them he will never feel like a human being, and the Snow Queen will always maintain her influence over him."

"But can you not give something to little Gerda whereby she may overcome all these evil influences?"

"I can give her no power so great as that which she already possesses. Her power is greater than ours, because it proceeds from her heart, from her being a loving and innocent child. If this power which she already possesses cannot give her access to the Snow Queen's palace and enable her to free Kay's eye and heart from the glass fragment, we can do nothing for her! Two miles hence is the Snow Queen's garden; thither you can carry the little maiden. Put her down close by the bush bearing red berries and half covered with snow: lose no time, and hasten back!"

Then the wise woman lifted Gerda on the reindeer's back, and away they urent.

"Oh, I have left my boots behind! I have left my gloves behind!" cried little Gerda, when it was too late. The cold was piercing, but the reindeer dared not stop; on he ran until he reached the bush with the red berries. Here he set Gerda aoun, kissed her, the tears rolling down his cheeks the while, and ran fast back again—which was the best thing he could do. And there stood poor Gerda, without shoes, without gloves, alone in that barren region, that terribly icy-cold Finland.

She ran on as fast as she could. A whole regiment of snowflakes came to meet her. They did not fall from the sky, which was cloudless and bright with the Northern Lights; then ran straight along the ground, and the farther Gerda advanced the larger they grew. Gerda then remembered how large and curious the snowflakes had appeared to her when one day she had looked at them through a burning-glass. These, however, were very much larger:

they were living forms; they were, in fact, the Snow Queen's guards. Their shapes were the strangest that could be imagined. Some looked like great ugly porcupines, others like snakes rolled into knots with their heads peering forth, and others like little fat bears with bristling hair. Little Gerda began to repeat "Our Father." Meanwhile it was so cold that she could see her own breath, which, as it escaped her mouth, ascended into the air like vapour. The cold grew intense, the vapour more dense, and at length took the forms of little bright angels which, as they touched the earth, became larger and more distinct. They wore helmets on their heads, and carried shields and spears in their hands; their number increased so rapidly that, by the time Gerda had finished her prayer, a whole legion stood around her. They thrust with their spears against the horrible snowflakes, which fell into thousands of pieces, and little Gerda walked on unhurt and undaunted. The angels touched her hands and feet, and then she scarcely felt the cold, and boldly approached the Snow Queen's palace.

But before we accompany her there, let us see what Kay is doing. He is certainly not thinking of little Gerda, least of all can he imagine that she is now standing at the palace gate.

THE SNOW QUEEN'S PALACE

The walls of the palace were formed of the driven snow,

its doors and windows of the cutting winds. There were above a hundred halls, the largest of them many miles in extent, all illuminated by the Northern Lights, all alike vast, empty, icily cold, and dazzlingly white. In the midst of the empty, interminable snow saloon lay a frozen lake; it was broken into a thousand pieces, but these pieces so exactly resembled each other that the breaking of them might well be deemed a work of more than human skill. The Snow Queen, when at home, always sat in the centre of this lake.

Little Kay was quite blue, nay, almost black with cold, but he did not observe it, for the Snow Queen had kissed away the shrinking feeling he used to experience, and his heart was like a lump of ice. He was busied among the sharp icy fragments, laying and joining them together in every possible way, just as people do with what are called Chinese puzzles. Kay could form the most curious and complete figures—and in his eyes these figures were of the utmost importance. He often formed whole words, but there was one word he could never succeed in form-ing—it was Eternity. The Snow Queen had said to him, "When you can put that figure together, you shall become your own master and I will give you the whole world, and a new pair of skates besides."

But he could never do it.

"Now I am going to the warm countries," said the Snow Queen. "I shall flit through the air, and look into the black cauldrons"—she meant the burning mountains

Etna and Vesuvius. "I shall whiten them a little; that will be good for the citrons and vineyards." So away flew the Snow Queen, leaving Kay sitting all alone in the large empty hall of ice.

He looked at the fragments, and thought and thought till his head ached. He sat so still and so stiff that one might have fancied that he too was frozen.

Cold and cutting blew the winds when little Gerda passed through the palace gates, but she repeated her evening prayer, and they immediately sank to rest. She entered the large, cold, empty hall; she saw Kay, she recognised him, she flew to him and fell upon his neck, she held him fast, and cried, "Kay! dear, dear Kay! I have found you at last!"

But he sat still as before—cold, silent, motionless. His unkindness wounded poor Gerda deeply. Hot and bitter were the tears she shed; they fell upon his breast, they reached his heart, they thawed the ice and dissolved the tiny splinter of glass within it. He looked at her whilst she sang her hymn—

> Our roses bloom and fade away.
> Our Infant Lord abides alway.
> May we be blessed His face to see,
> And ever little children be.

Then Kay burst into tears. He wept till the glass splinter floated in his eye and well with his tears; he knew his old companion immediately, and exclaimed with joy, "Gerda, my dear little Gerda, where have you been all this time?—and where have I been?"

He looked around him. "How cold it is here! how wide and empty!" Then he embraced Gerda, whilst she laughed and wept by turns. Even the pieces of ice took part in their joy; they danced about merrily, and when they were wearied and lay down they formed of their own accord the mystical letters of which the Snow Queen had said that when Kay could put them together he should be his own master, and that she would give him the whole world, with a new-pair of skates besides.

And Gerda kissed his cheeks, whereupon they became fresh and glowing as ever; she kissed his eyes, and they sparkled like her own; she kissed his hands and feet, and he was once more healthy and merry. The Snow Queen might now come home as soon as she liked—it mattered not; Kay's charter of freedom stood written on the lake in bright icy characters.

They took each other by the hand, and wandered forth out of the palace; and as they walked on, the winds were hushed into a calm, and the sun burst forth in splendour from among the dark storm-clouds. When they arrived at the bush with the red berries, they found the reindeer standing by awaiting their arrival; he had brought with him another and younger reindeer, whose udders were full, and who gladly gave her warm milk to refresh the young travellers.

The old reindeer and the young hind now carried Kay and Gerda on their backs, first to the little hot room of the wise woman of Finland, where they warmed themselves, and received advice how to proceed on their journey home, and afterwards to the abode of the Lapland woman, who made them some new clothes and provided them with a sledge.

The whole party now ran on together till they came to the boundary of the country; but just where the green leaves began to sprout, the Lapland woman and the two reindeers took their leave. "Farewell! farewell!" said they all. And the first little bird, they had seen for many a long day began to chirp, and warbie their pretty songs; and the trees of the forest burst upon them full of rich and variously tinted foliage. Suddenly the green boughs parted asunder, and a spirited horse galloped up. Gerda knew it well for it was one which had been harnessed to her gold coach; and on it sat a young girl wearing a bright scarlet cap, and with pistols on the holster before her. It was indeed no other than the robber-maiden, who, weary of her home in the forest, was going on her travels, first to the North and afterwards to other parts of the world. She at once recognised Gerda, and Gerda had not forgotten her. Most joyful was their greeting.

"A fine gentleman you are, to be sure, you graceless young truant!" said she to Kay. "I should like to know if you deserved that any one should be running to the end of the world on your account!"

But Gerda stroked her cheeks, and asked after the prince and princess.

"They are gone travelling into foreign countries," replied the robber-maiden.

"And the raven?" asked Gerda.

"Ah! the raven is dead," returned she. "The tame beloved has become a widow, so she hops about with a piece of worsted wound round her leg; she moans most piteously, and chatters more than ever! But tell me now all that has happened to you, and how you managed to pick up your old playfellow."

And Gerda and Kay told their story.

"Snip-snap-snurre-basselurre!" said the robber-maiden. She pressed the hands of both, promised that if ever she passed through their town she would pay them a visit, and then bade them farewell, and rode away out into the wide world.

Kay and Gerda walked on hand in hand, and wherever they went it was spring, beautiful spring, with its bright flowers and green leaves.

They arrived at a large town, the church bells were ringing merrily, and they immediately recognised the high towers rising into the sky—it was the town wherein they had lived. Joyfully they passed through the streets, and stopped at the door of Gerda's grandmother. They walked up the stairs and entered the well-known room. The clock said "Tick, tick!" and the hands moved as before. Only one alteration could they find, and that was in themselves, for they saw that they were now fullgrown persons. The rose-trees on the roof blossomed in front of the open window, and there beneath them stood the children's stools. Kay and Gerda went and sat down upon them, still holding each other by the hand; the cold, hollow splendour of the Snow Queen's palace they had forgotten, it seemed to them only an unpleasant dream. The grandmother meanwhile sat in the bright sunshine, and read from the Bible these words: "Unless ye become as little children, ye shall not enter into the kingdom of heaven."

And Kay and Gerda gazed on each other; they now understood the words of their hymn—

> Our roses bloom and fade away,
> Our Infant Lord abides alway;
> May we be blessed His face to see,
> And ever little children be!

THE GIFT OF THE MAGI

O. HENRY

ONE DOLLAR and eighty-seven cents. That was all. And sixty cents of it was in pennies. Pennies saved one and two at a time by bulldozing the grocer and the vegetable man and the butcher until one's cheeks burned with the silent imputation of parsimony that such close dealing implied. Three times Della counted it. One dollar and eighty-seven cents. And the next day would be Christmas.

There was clearly nothing to do but flop down on the shabby little couch and howl. So Della did it. Which instigates the moral reflection that life is made up of sobs, sniffles, and smiles, with sniffles predominating.

While the mistress of the home is gradually subsiding from the first stage to the second, take a look at the home. A furnished flat at $8 per week. It did not exactly beggar description, but it certainly had that word on the lookout for the mendicancy squad.

In the vestibule below was a letter-box into which no letter would go. and an electric button from which no mortal finger could coax; a ring. Also appertaining thereunto was a card bearing the name "Mr. James Dillingham Young."

The "Dillingham" had been flung to the breeze during a former period of prosperity when its possessor was being paid $30 per week. Now, when the income was shrunk to $20, the letters of "Dillingham" looked blurred, as though they were thinking seriously of contracting to a modest and unassuming D. But whenever Mr. James Dillingham Young came home and reached his flat above he was called "Jim" and greatly hugged by Mrs. James Dillingham Young, already introduced to you as Della. Which is all very good.

Della finished her cry and attended to her cheeks with the powder rag. She stood by the window and looked out dully at a grey cat walking a grey fence in a grey backyard. Tomorrow would be Christmas Day. and she had only $1.87 with which to buy Jim a present. She had been saving every penny she could for months, with this result. Twenty dollars a week doesn't go far. Expenses had been greater than she had calculated. They always are. Only $1.87 to buy a present for Jim. Her Jim. Many a happy hour she had spent planning for something nice for him. Something fine and rare and sterling—something just a little bit near to being worthy of the honour of being owned by Jim.

There was a pier-glass between the windows of the room. Perhaps you have seen a pier-glass in an $8 flat. A very thin and very agile person may, by observing his reflection in a rapid sequence of longitudinal strips. obtain a fairly accurate conception of his looks. Della, being, slender, had mastered the art.

Suddenly she whirled from the window and stood before the glass. Her eyes were shining brilliantly but her face had lost its colour within twenty seconds. Rapidly she pulled down her hair and let it fall to its full length.

Now, there were two possessions of the James Dillingham Youngs in which they both took a mighty pride. One was Jim's gold watch that had been his fathers and his grandfathers. The other was Della's hair. Had the Queen of Sheba lived in the flat across the airshaft, Della would have let her hair hang out the window some day to dry just to depreciate Her Majesty's jewels and gifts. Had King Solomon been the janitor with all his Treasures piled up in the basement, Jim would have pulled out his watch every time he passed. just to see him pluck at his beard from envy.

So now Della's beautiful hair fell about her, rippling and shining like a cascade of brown waters. It reached below her knee and made itself almost a garment for her. And then she did it up again nervously and quickly. Once she faltered for a minute and stood still while a tear or two splashed on the worn red carpet.

On went her old brown jacket; on went her old brown hat. With a whirl of skirts and with the brilliant sparkle still in her eyes, she fluttered out the door and down the stairs to the street.

Where she stopped the sign read: "Mme Sofronie. Hair Goods of All Kinds." One flight up Della ran, and collected herself, panting. Madame, large, too white, chilly hardly looked the "Sofronie."

"Will you buy my hair?" asked Della.

"I buy hair," said Madame. "Take yer hat off and let's have a sight at the looks of it."

Down rippled the brown cascade.

"Twenty dollars," said Madame, lifting the mass with a practised hand.

"Give it to me quick," said Della.

Oh, and the next two hours tripped by on rosy wings. Forget the hashed metaphor. She was ransacking the stores for Jim's present.

She found it at last. It surely had been made for Jim and no one else. There was no other like it in any of the stores, and she had turned all of them inside out. It was a platinum fob chain simple and chaste in design, properly proclaiming its value by substance alone and not by meretricious ornamentation—as all good things should do. It was even worthy of The Watch. As soon as she saw it she knew that it must be Jim's. It was like him. Quietness and value—the description applied to both. Twenty one dollars they took from her for it and she hurried home with the 87 cents. With that chain on his watch Jim might be properly anxious about the time in any company. Grand as the watch was, he sometimes looked at it on the sly on account of the old leather strap that he used in place of a chain.

When Della reached home her intoxication gave way to a little to prudence and reason. She got out her curling irons and lighted the gas and went to work repairing the ravages made by generosity added to love. Which is always a tremendous task, dear friends—a mammoth task.

Within forty minutes her head was covered with tiny, close-lying curls that made her look wonderfully like a truant schoolboy. She looked at her reflection in the mirror long, carefully, and critically.

"If Jim doesn't kill me," she said to herself, "before he takes a second look at me, he'll say I look like a Coney Island chorus girl. But that could I do—oh! what could I do with a dollar and eighty seven cents?"

At seven o'clock the coffee was made and the frying-pan was on the back of the stove, hot and ready to cook the chops.

Jim was never late. Della doubled the fob chain in her hand and sat on the corner of the table near the door that he always entered. Then she heard his step on the stair away down on the first flight, and she turned while for just a moment. She had a habit of saying little silent prayers about the simplest everyday things, and now she whispered: "Please God, make him think I am still pretty."

The door opened and Jim stepped in and closed it. He looked thin and very serious. Poor fellow, he was only twenty-two and to be burdened with a family! He needed a new overcoat and he was without gloves.

Jim stopped inside the door, as immovable as a setter at the scent of quail. His eyes were fixed upon Della, and there was an expression in them that she could not read, and it terrified her. It was not anger nor surprise, nor disapproval, nor horror, nor anger of the sentiments that she had been prepared for. He simply stared at her fixedly with that peculiar expression on his face.

Della wriggled off the table and went for him.

"Jim darling," she cried. "don't look at me that way. I had my hair cut off and sold it because I couldn't have lived through Christmas without giving you a present. It'll grow out again—you won't mind will you? I just had to do it. My hair grows awfully fast. Say Merry Christmas! Jim, and lets be happy you don't know what a nice—what a beautiful, nice gift I've got for you."

"You've cut off your hair?" asked Jim, laboriously as if he had not arrived at that patent fact yet even after the hardest mental labour.

"Cut it off and sold it", said Della. "Don't you like me just as well anyhow? I'm me without my hair. ain't I?"

Jim looked about the room curiously.

"You say your hair is gone?" he said, with an air almost of idiocy.

"You needn't look for it," said Della. "It's sold. I tell you—sold and gone too. It's Christmas Eve, boy. Be good to me, for it went for you. Maybe the hairs of my head were numbered," she went on with a sudden serious sweetness, "but nobody could ever count my love for you. Shall I put the chops on, Jim?"

Out of his trance Jim seemed quickly to wake. He enfolded his Della. For ten seconds let us regard with discreet scrutiny some inconsequential object in the other direction. Eight dollars a week or a million a year—what is the difference? A mathematician or a wit would give you the wrong answer. The magi brought valuable gifts, but that was not among them. This dark assertion will be illuminated later on.

Jim drew a package from his overcoat pocket and threw it upon the table.

"Don't make any mistake, Dell," he said, "about me. I don't think there's anything in the way of a haircut or a shave or a shampoo that could make me like my girl any less. But if you'll unwrap that package you may see why you had me going a while at first."

White fingers and nimble tore at the string and paper. And then an ecstatic scream of joy; and then alas! a quick feminine change to hysterical tears and wails, necessitating the immediate employment of all the comforting powers of the lord of the flat.

For there lay The Combs—the set of combs, side and back, that Della had worshipped for long in a Broadway window. Beautiful combs, pure tortoise shell with jewelled rims—just the shade to wear in the beautiful vanished hair. They were expensive combs, she knew, and her heart had simply craved and yearned over them without the least hope of possession. And now, they were hers, but the tresses that should have adorned the covered adornments were gone.

But she hugged them to her bosom, and at length she was able to look up with dim eyes and a smile and say: "My hair grows so fast, Jim!"

And then Della leaped up like a little singed cat and cried, "Oh, oh!"

Jim had not yet seen his beautiful present. She held it out to him eagerly upon her open palm. The dull precious metal seemed to flash with a reflection of her bright and ardent spirit.

"Isn't it a dandy, Jim? I hunted all over town to find it. You'll have to look at the time a hundred times a day now. Give me your watch. I want to see how it looks on it."

Instead of obeying. Jim tumbled down on the couch and put his hands under the back of his head and smiled.

"Dell," said he, "let's put our Christmas presents away and keep 'em a while. They're too nice to use just at present. I sold the watch to get the money to buy your combs. And now suppose you put the chops on."

The magi, as you know, were wise men—wonderfully wise men—who brought gifts to the Babe in the manger. They invented the art of giving Christmas presents. Being wise, their gifts were no doubt wise ones, possibly bearing the privilege of exchange in case of duplication. And here I have lamely related to you the uneventful chronicle of two foolish children in a flat who most unwisely sacrificed for each other the greatest treasures of their houses.

But in a last word to the wise of these days let it be said that all who give gifts these two were the wisest. Of all who give and receive gifts, such as they are wisest. Everywhere they are wisest. They are the magi.

The Gift of the Magi

A Christmas Story

A CHRISTMAS STORY

"HUSH! Hurrah!" said the Green Goblin, and he stole Marjorie's doll.

"Ha, ha!" gurgled the Silver Fairy and *he* stole the holly.

"Woof!" whispered Greylegs, and he pulled Pussy's tail.

For Marjorie was too busy reading, just as you are, and Billy and Tots were listening very hard.

But, if you think you may keep the doll, Green Goblin, you're mistaken.

And *you* mayn't keep the holly, Master Silver Fairy.

And you'd better stop pulling Pussy's tail, Greylegs.

For everybody simply *must* be good at Christmas-time.

THE FIR-TREE

HANS CHRISTIAN ANDERSEN

FAR AWAY in the deep forest there once grew a pretty Fir-Tree. The sun shone full upon him, the breeze played freely around him, and in the neighbourhood grew many companion fir-trees, some older, some younger. But the little Fir-Tree was not happy: he was always longing to be tall; he thought not of the warm sun and the fresh air; he cared not for the merry, prattling peasant children who came to the forest to look for strawberries and raspberries,—except indeed, some-times, when after having filled their pitchers, or threaded the bright berries on a straw, they would sit down near the little Fir-Tree and say, "What a pretty little tree this is!" and then the Fir-Tree would feel very much vexed.

"Oh that I were as tall as the others," sighed the little Tree, "then I should spread out my branches so far, and my crown should look out over the wide world around! the birds would build their nests among my branches, and when the wind blew I should bend my head so grandly, just as the others do!" He had no pleasure in the sunshine, in the song of the birds, or in the red clouds that sailed over him every morning and evening.

In the wintertime, when the ground was covered with the white glistening snow, there was a hare that would come continually scampering about, and jumping right over the little Tree's head—and that was most provoking! However, two winters passed away, and by the third the Tree was so tall that the hare was obliged to run round it "Oh! to grow, to grow, to become tall and old, that is the only thing in the world worth living for" So thought the Tree.

The woodcutters came in the autumn and felled some among the largest of the trees. This happened every year, and our young fir, who was by this time a good height shuddered when he saw those grand, magnificent trees fall with a tremendous crash crackling to the earth. Their boughs were then all cut off; terribly naked and lanky and long did the stem look after this—they could hardly be recognised. They were laid one upon another in waggons, and horses drew them away, far, far away from the forest.

Where could they be going? What might be their fortunes?

Next spring, when the swallows and the storks had returned from abroad, the Fir asked them if they knew whither the felled trees had been taken.

The swallows knew nothing about the matter; but the stork looked thoughtful for a moment, then nodded his head and said, "Yes, I believe I have seen them! As I was flying from Egypt to this place I met several ships; those ships had splendid masts. I have little doubt that they were the trees that you speak of, they smelled like fir-wood. I may congratulate you, for they sailed gloriously, quite gloriously!"

"Oh that I too were tall enough to sail upon the sea! Tell me what it is, this sea, and what it looks like."

"Thank you, it would take too long, a great deal!" said the stork, and away he stalked.

"Rejoice in your youth!" said the sunbeams; "rejoice in your luxuriant youth, in the fresh life that is within you!"

And the wind kissed the Tree, and the dew wept tears over him, but the Fir-Tree understood them not.

When Christmas approached, many quite young trees were felled, trees which were some of them not so tall or of just the same height as the young restless Fir-Tree who was always longing to be away. These young trees were chosen from the most beautiful. Their branches were not cut off; they were laid in a waggon, and horses drew them away, far, far away from the forest

"Where are they going?" asked the Fir-Tree. "They are not larger than I am, indeed one of them was much less. Why do they keep all their branches? Where can they be gone?"

"We know! we know!" twittered the sparrows. "We peeped in through the windows of the town below! We know where they are gone. Oh, you cannot think what honour and glory they receive! We looked through the windowpanes and saw them planted in a warm room, and decked out with such beautiful things, gilded apples, sweetmeats, playthings, and hundreds of bright candles!"

"And then?" asked the Fir-Tree, trembling in every bough; "and then? What happened then?"

"Oh, we saw no more. That was beautiful, beautiful beyond compare!"

"Is this glorious lot destined to be mine?" cried the Fir-Tree with delight. "This is far better than sailing over the sea. How I long for the time. Oh that Christmas were come! I am now tall and have many branches, like the others which last year were carried away. Oh that I were even now in the waggon! that I were in the warm room, honoured and adorned! and then yes, then, something still better must happen, else why should they take the trouble to decorate me? It must be that something still greater, still more splendid, must happen—but what? Oh I suffer, I suffer with longing! I know not what it is that I feel."

"Rejoice in our love!" said the air and the sunshine. "Rejoice in your youth and your freedom!"

But rejoice he never would. He grew and grew, in winter as in summer; he stood there clothed in green, dark green foliage. The people that saw him said, "That is a beautiful tree!" and next Christmas he was the first that was felled. The axe struck sharply through the wood, the Tree fell to the earth with a heavy groan; he suffered an agony, a faintness that he had never expected. He quite forgot to think of his good fortune, he felt such sorrow at being compelled to leave his home, the place whence he had sprung. He knew that he would never see again those dear old comrades, or the little bushes and flowers that had flourished under his shadow, perhaps not even the birds. Neither did he find the journey by any means pleasant.

The Tree first came to himself when in the courtyard to which he was first taken with the other trees, he heard a man say, "This is a splendid one, the very thing we want!"

Then came two smartly-dressed servants, and carried the Fir-Tree into a large and handsome saloon. Pictures hung on the walls, and on the mantelpiece stood large Chinese vases with lions on the lids. There were rocking-chairs, silken sofas, tables covered with picture-books, and toys. And the Fir-Tree was planted in a large cask filled with sand; but no one could know that it was a cask, for it was hung with green cloth and placed upon a carpet woven of many gay colours. Oh, how the Tree trembled! what was to happen next? A young lady, assisted by the servants, now began to adorn him. Upon some branches they hung little nets cut out of coloured paper, every net filled with sugar plums; from others gilded apples and walnuts were suspended, looking just as if they had grown there, and more than a hundred little wax tapers, red, blue, and white, were placed here and there among the boughs. Dolls that looked almost like men and women the Tree had never seen such things before—seemed dancing to and fro among the leaves, and highest, on the summit was fastened a large star of gold tinsel. This was indeed splendid. splendid beyond compare.

"This evening," they said, "this evening it will be lighted up."

"Would that it were evening," thought the Tree. "Would that the lights were kindled, for then,—what will happen then? Will the trees come out of the forest to see me? Will the sparrows fly here and look in through the window panes? Shall I stand here adorned both winter and summer?"

He thought much of it; he thought till he had barkache with longing, and barkaches with trees are as bad as head-aches with us.

The candles were lighted—oh, what a blaze of splendour! The Tree trembled in all his branches so that one of them caught fire. "Oh dear!" cried the young lady, and it was extinguished in great haste.

So the Tree dared not tremble again; he was so fearful of losing something of his splendour. He felt almost bewildered in the midst of all this glory and brightness. And now, all of a sudden, both folding-doors were flung open, and a troop of children rushed in as if they had a mind to jump over him; the older people followed more quietly. The little ones stood quite silent, but only for a moment. Then their jubilee burst forth afresh. They shouted till the calls re-echoed, they danced round the Tree, one present after another was torn down.

"What are they doing?" thought the Tree. "What will

happen now?" The candles burnt down to the branches, so they were extinguished, and the children were given leave to plunder the Tree. They rushed upon him in such riot that the boughs all crackled; had not his summit been festooned with the gold star to the ceiling he would have been overturned.

The children danced and played about with their beautiful playthings; no one thought of the Tree any more except the old nurse. She came and peeped among the boughs, but it was only to see whether, perchance, a fig or an apple had not been left among them.

"A story! a story!" cried the children, pulling a short thick man towards the Tree. He sat down saying, "It is pleasant to sit under the shade of green boughs; besides, the tree may be benefited by hearing my story. But I shall only tell you one. Would you like to hear about Ivedy Avedy or about Humpty Dumpty, who fell downstairs, and yet came to the throne and won the Princess?"

"Ivedy Avedy!" cried some; "Humpty Dumpty!" cried others. There was a great uproar. The Fir-Tree alone was silent, thinking to himself, "Ought I to make a noise as they do? or ought I to do nothing at all?" For he most certainly was one of the company, and had done all that had been required of him.

And the short thick man told the story of Humpty Dumpty who fell downstairs, and yet came to the throne and won the Princess. And the children clapped their hands and called out for another; they wanted to hear the story of Ivedy Avedy also, but they did not get it. The Fir-Tree stood meanwhile quite silent and thoughtful, the birds in the forest had never related anything like this. "Humpty Dumpty fell downstairs, and yet was raised to the throne and won the Princess! Yes, yes, strange things come to pass in the world!" thought the Fir-Tree, who believed it must all be true, because such a pleasant man had related it. "Who knows but I may fall downstairs and win a Princess?" And he rejoiced in the expectation of being next day again decked out with candles and playthings, gold and fruit. "Tomorrow I will not tremble," thought he. "I will rejoice in my magnificence. Tomorrow I shall again hear the story of Humpty Dumpty, and perhaps that about Ivedy Avedy likewise." And the Tree mused upon this all night.

In the morning the maids came in. "Now begins my state anew!" thought the Tree. But they dragged him out of the room, up the stairs, and into an attic chamber, and there thrust him into a dark corner where not a ray of light could penetrate. "What can be the meaning of this?" thought the Tree. "What am I to do here? What shall I hear in this place?" And he leant against the wall, and thought, and thought. And plenty of time he had for thinking it over, for day after day, and night after night passed away, and yet no one ever came into the room. At last somebody did come in, but it was only to push into the corner some old trunks. The Tree was now entirely hidden from sight and apparently quite forgotten.

"It is now winter," thought the Tree. "The ground is hard and covered with snow; they cannot plant me now, so I am to stay here in shelter till the spring. Men are so prudent! I only wish it were not so dark and so dreadfully lonely!"

"Squeak! squeak!" cried a little mouse, just then gliding forward. Another followed; they snuffed about the Fir-Tree, and then slipped in and out among the branches.

"It is horribly cold!" said the little mice. "Otherwise it is very comfortable here. Don't you think so, you old Fir-Tree?"

"I am not old," said the Fir-Tree; "there are many who are much older than I."

"How came you here?" asked the mice, "and what do you know?" They were most uncommonly curious. "Tell us about the most delightful place on earth? Have you ever been there? Have you been into the storeroom, where cheeses lie on the shelves, and bacon hangs from the ceiling; where one can dance over tallow-candles; where one goes in thin and comes out fat?"

"I know nothing about that," said the Tree, "but I know the forest, where the sun shines and where the birds sing!" And then he spoke of his youth and its pleasures. The little mice had never heard anything like it before. They listened very attentively and said, "Well, to be sure! How much you have seen! How happy you have been!"

"Happy!" repeated the Fir-Tree, in surprise, and he thought a moment over all that he had been saying,—

"yes, on the whole those were pleasant times!" He then told them about the Christmas Eve when he had been decked out with cakes and candles.

"Oh!" cried the little mice, "how happy you have been, you old Fir-Tree!"

"I am not old at all!" returned the Fir. "It was only this winter that I left the forest; I am just in the prime of life!"

"How well you can talk!" said the little mice, and the next night they came again and brought with them four other little mice, who wanted also to hear the Tree's history. And the more the Tree spoke of his youth in the forest, the more vividly he remembered it, and said, "Yes, those were pleasant times! but they may come again, they may come again! Humpty Dumpty fell downstairs, and yet for all that he won the Princess; perhaps I, too, may win a princess!" And then the Fir-Tree thought of a pretty little delicate birch-tree that grew in the forest, a real princess, a very lovely princess was she to the Fir-Tree.

"Who is this Humpty Dumpty?" asked the little mice. Whereupon he related the tale; he could remember every word of it perfectly; and the little mice were ready to jump to the top of the Tree for joy. The night following several more mice came, and on Sunday came also two rats. They, however, declared that the story was not at all amusing, which much vexed the little mice, who, after hearing their opinion, could not like it so well either.

"Do you know only that one story?" asked the rats.

"Only that one!" answered the Tree. "I heard it on the

happiest evening of my life, though I did not then know how happy I was."

"It is a miserable story! Do you know none about pork and tallow? No storeroom story?"

"No," said the Tree.

"Well, then, we have heard enough of it!" returned the rats, and they went their ways.

The little mice, too, never came again. The Tree sighed, "It was pleasant when they sat round me, those busy little mice, listening to my words. Now that, too, is all past! However, I shall have pleasure in remembering it, when I am taken from this place."

But when would that be? One morning, people came and routed out the lumber-room. The trunks were taken away, the Tree, too, was dragged out of the corner. They threw him carelessly on the floor, but one of the servants picked him up and carried him downstairs. Once more he beheld the light of day. "Now life begins again!" thought the Tree. He felt the fresh air, the warm sunbeams—he was out in the court. All happened so quickly that the Tree quite forgot to look at himself,—there was so much to look at all around. The court joined a garden. Everything was so fresh and blooming, the roses clustered so bright and so fragrant round the trelliswork, the lime-trees were in full blossom, and the swallows flew backwards and forwards, twittering.

"I shall live! I shall live!" He was filled with delightful hope; he tried to spread out his branches,—but alas! they were all dried up and yellow. He was thrown down upon a heap of weeds and nettles. The star of gold tinsel that had been left fixed on his crown now sparkled brightly in the sunshine. Some merry children were playing in the court, the same who at Christmas-time had danced round the Tree. One of the youngest now perceived the gold star, and ran to tear it off.

"Look at it, still fastened to the ugly old Christmas Tree!" cried he, trampling upon the boughs till they broke under his boots.

And the Tree looked on all the flowers of the garden now blooming in the freshness of their beauty; he looked upon himself, and he wished from his heart that he had been left to wither alone in the dark corner of the lumber-room. He called to mind his happy forest life, the merry Christmas Eve, and the little mice who had listened so eagerly when he related the story of Humpty Dumpty.

"Past, all past!" said the poor Tree. "Had I but been happy, as I might have been! Past, all past!"

And the servant came and broke the Tree into small pieces, heaped them up and set fire to them. And the Tree groaned deeply, and every groan sounded like a little shot. The children all ran up to the place and jumped about in front of the blaze. But at each of those heavy groans the Fir-Tree thought of a bright summer's day, or a starry winter's night in the forest, of Christmas Eve, or of Humpty Dumpty, the only story that he knew and could relate. And at last the Tree was burned.

The boys played about in the court. On the bosom of the youngest sparkled the gold star that the Tree had worn on the happiest evening of his life; but that was past, and the Tree was past and the story also, past! past! for all stories must come to an end some time or other.

FRIENDSHIP

SANTA CLAUS came here last night,
  Came softly without knocking;
He brought a Doll for little May,
  And pinned it to her Stocking.

Little May bounced out of Bed;
  Clasped gaily her new Dolly;
And as she kissed and called it Sweet,
  Forgot her old Dolls wholly.

Sally Rag, her old plain friend,
  No more gifts or graces;
All day she praised Aminta's charms,
  And hugged Aminta's laces.

Little May now lies in Bed;
  But e'er she sought Dream Valley,
She flung Aminta on the Floor—
  And went to sleep with Sally!

A Christmas Memory

I THINK that Dick must have had a wise fairy god-mother, who gave him one of her very best gifts. This gift was a good memory for nice things. Dick was nearly always happy, because he could always remember something nice that had happened to him. When some children would be quarrelsome and naughty, because they had nothing to do, Dick would be quite happy thinking over some jolly day he had had.

For some time after Dick had measles, he was not allowed to go out to play with his friends, and now and then he got tired of playing with his toys. Then he would just sit down and rest, and think about every jolly Christmas that he could remember.

A Christmas Memory

Christmas Windows

CHRISTMAS WINDOWS

THE Christmas windows are lovely and bright,
   All filled with wonderful toys,
   Meant for the pleasure and sole delight
Of nice little girls and boys.

"If you were rich, now what would you do?"
   Says Joan to her sister small.
"I'd buy every toy and I'd give them to you
   And then I could play with them all."

A Christmas Visitor

ANON

HE COMES in the night! he comes in the night!
  He softly, silently comes;
  While the little brown heads on the pillows so white
  Are dreaming of bugles and drums.

He cuts through the snow like a ship through the foam,
  While the white flakes around him whirl;
Who tells him I know not, but he findeth the home
  Of each good little boy and girl.

His sleigh it is long, and deep and wide;
  It will carry a host of things,
While dozens of drums hang over the side,
  With the sticks sticking, under the strings.

And yet not the sound of a drum is heard,
  Not a bugle blast is blown,
As he mounts to the chimney-top like a bird,
  And drops to the hearth like a stone.

The little red stockings he silently fills,
  Till the stockings will hold no more;
The bright little sleds for the great snow hills
  Are quickly set down on the floor.

Then Santa Claus mounts to the roof like a bird,
  And glides to his seat in the sleigh;
Not the sound of a bugle or drum is heard
  As he noiselessly gallops away.

He rides to the East, and he rides to the West,
  Of his goodies he touches not one;
He eateth the crumbs of the Christmas feast
  When the dear little folks are done.

Old Santa Claus doeth all that he can;
  This beautiful mission is his;
Then, children, be good to the little old man
  When you find who the little man is.

The Christmas Dinner

Washington Irving

HE DINNER was served up in the great hall, where the squire always held his Christmas banquet. A blazing, crackling fire of logs had been heaped on to warm the spacious apartment, and the flame went sparkling and wreathing up the wide-mouthed chimney. The great picture of the crusader and his white horse had been profusely decorated with greens for the occasion; and holly and ivy had likewise been wreathed round the helmet and weapons on the opposite wall, which I understand were the arms of the same warrior. A sideboard was set out just under this chivalric trophy, on which was a display of plate that might have vied (at least in variety) with Belshazzar's parade of the vessels of the temple: 'flagons, cans, cups, beakers, goblets, basins, and ewers'; the gorgeous utensils of good companionship that had gradually accumulated through many generations of jovial housekeepers. Before these stood the two Yule candles, beaming like two stars of the first magnitude; other lights were distributed in branches, and the whole array glittered like a firmament of silver.

The parson said grace, which was not a short familiar one, such as is commonly addressed to the Deity in these unceremonious days; but a long courtly, well-worded one of the ancient school. There was now a pause, as if something was expected; when suddenly the butler entered the hall with some degree of bustle: he was attended by a servant on each side with a large wax-light and bore a silver dish, on which was an enormous pig's head, decorated with rosemary, with a lemon in its mouth, which was placed with great formality at the head of the table. The moment this pageant made its appearance, the harper struck up a flourish; at the conclusion of which a young Oxonian, on receiving a hint from the squire, gave, with an air of the most comic gravity, an old carol, the first verse of which was as follows:

> *Caput apri defero,*
> *Reddens laudes Domino.*
> *The boar's head in hand bring I,*
> *With garlands gay and rosemary.*
> *I pray you all synge merily*
> *Qui estis in convivio.*

Though prepared to witness many of these little eccentricities, from being apprized of the peculiar hobby of mine host; yet, I confess, the parade with which so odd a dish was introduced somewhat perplexed me, until I gathered from the conversation of the squire and the parson, that it was meant to represent the bringing in of the boar's head; a dish formerly served up with much ceremony and the sound of minstrelsy and song, at great tables, on Christmas day. "I like the old custom," said the squire, "not merely because it is stately and pleasing in itself, but because it was observed at the college at Oxford at which I was educated. When I hear the old song chanted, it brings back to mind the time when I was young and gamesome—and the noble old college hall—and my fellow-students loitering about in their black gowns; many of whom, poor lads, are now in their graves!"

The table was literally loaded with good cheer, and presented an epitome of country abundance, in this season of overflowing larders. A distinguished post was allotted to "ancient sirloin", as mine host termed it; being, as he added, "the standard of old English hospitality, and a joint of goodly presence, and full of expectation". There were several dishes quaintly decorated, and which had evidently something traditional in their embellishments; but about which, as I did not like to appear overcurious, I asked no questions.

I could not, however, but notice a pie, magnificently decorated with peacocks' feathers, in the imitation of the tail of that bird, which overshadowed a considerable tract of the table. This, the squire confessed, with some little hesitation, was a pheasant pie, though a peacock pie was certainly the most authentical; but there had been such a mortality among the peacocks this season, that he could not prevail upon himself to have one killed.

When the cloth was removed, the butler brought in a huge silver vessel of rare and curious workmanship, which he placed before the squire. Its appearance was hailed with acclamation; being the Wassail Bowl, so renowned in Christmas festivity. The contents had been prepared by the squire himself; for it was a beverage in the skilful mixture of which he particularly prided himself; alleging that it was too abstruse and complex for the comprehension of an ordinary servant. It was a potation, indeed, that might well make the heart of a toper leap within him; being composed of the richest and raciest wines, highly spiced and sweetened, with roasted apples bobbing about the surface.

The old gentleman's whole countenance beamed with a serene look of indwelling light, as he stirred this mighty bowl. Having raised it to his lips, with a hearty wish of a merry Christmas to all present, he sent it brimming round the board, for everyone to follow his example, according to the primitive style; pronouncing it "the ancient fountain of good-feeling, where all hearts met together".

There was much laughing and rallying as the honest emblem of Christmas joviality circulated, and was kissed rather coyly by the ladies. When it reached Master Simon, he raised it in both hands, and with the air of a boon companion struck up an old Wassail chanson.

When the ladies had retired, the conversation, as usual,

became still more animated; many good things were broached which had been thought of during dinner, but which would not exactly do for a lady's ear; and though I cannot positively affirm that there was much wit uttered, yet I have certainly heard many contests of rare wit produce much less laughter. Wit, after all, is a mighty, tart, pungent, ingredient, and much too acid for some stomachs; but honest good humour is the oil and wine of a merry meeting, and there is no jovial companionship equal to that where jokes are rather small, and laughter abundant.

The squire told several long stories of early college pranks and adventures, in some of which the parson had been a sharer; though in looking at the latter, it required some effort of imagination to figure such a little dark anatomy of a man into the perpetrator of a madcap gambol.

I found the tide of wine and wassail fast gaining on the dry land of sober judgement. The company grew merrier and louder as their jokes grew duller. Master Simon was in as chirping a humour as a grasshopper filled with dew; his old songs grew of a warmer complexion, and he began to talk maudlin. He even gave a long song about the wooing of a widow.

This song inspired a fat-headed old gentleman, who made several attempts to tell rather a broad story out of Joe Miller, that was pat to the purpose; but he always stuck in the middle, everybody recollecting the latter part excepting himself. The parson, too, began to show the effects of good cheer, having gradually settled down into a doze, and his wig sitting most suspiciously on one side. Just at this juncture we were summoned to the drawing-room, and I suspect, at the private instigation of mine host, whose joviality seemed always tempered with a proper love of decorum.

After the dinner table was removed, the hall was given up to the youngest members of the family, who, prompted to all kinds of noisy mirth by the Oxonian and Master Simon, made its old walls ring with their merriment, as they played at romping games. I delight in the witnessing the gambols of children, and particularly at this happy holiday season, and could not help stealing out of the drawing-room on hearing one of their peals of laughter. I found them at the game of blind-man's-buff.

Master Simon, who was the leader of their revels, and seemed on all occasions to fulfil the office of that ancient potentate, the Lord of Misrule, was blinded in the midst of the hall. The little beings were as busy about him as the mock fairies about Falstaff; pinching him, plucking at the skirts of his coat, and tickling him with straws. One fine blue-eyed girl of about thirteen, with her flaxen hair all in beautiful confusion, her frolic face in a glow, her frock half torn off her shoulders, a complete picture of a romp, was the chief tormentor; and, from the slyness with which Master Simon avoided the smaller game, and hemmed this wild little nymph in corners, and obliged her to jump shrieking over chairs, I suspected the rogue of being not a whit more blinded than was convenient.

When I returned to the drawing-room, I found the company seated round the fire listening to the parson, who gave several anecdotes of the fancies of the neighbouring peasantry, concerning the effigy of the crusader, which lay on the tomb by the church altar. As it was the only monument of the kind in that part of the country, it had always been regarded with feelings of superstition by the good wives of the village. It was said to get up from the tomb and walk the rounds of the churchyard on stormy nights, particularly when it thundered; and one old woman whose cottage bordered on the churchyard, had seen it through the windows of the church, when the moon shone, slowly pacing up and down the aisles. It was the belief that some wrong had been left unredressed by the deceased, or some treasure hidden, which kept the spirit in a state of trouble and restlessness. Some talked of gold and jewels buried in the tomb, over which the spectre kept watch, and there was a story current of a sexton in old times who endeavoured to break his way to the coffin at night, but, just as he reached it, received a violent blow from the marble hand of the effigy, which stretched him senseless on the pavement. These tales were often laughed at by some of the sturdier among the rustics, yet when night came on, there were some of the stoutest unbelievers that were shy of venturing alone in the footpath that led across the churchyard.

Whilst we were all attention to the parson's stories, our ears were suddenly assailed by a burst of heterogeneous sounds from the hall. The door suddenly flew open, and a train came trooping into the room, that might have been mistaken for the breaking-up of the court of Fairy. That indefatigable spirit, Master Simon, in the faithful discharge of his duties as Lord of Misrule, had conceived the idea of a Christmas mummery or masking; and having called in to his assistance the Oxonian and a young officer, who were equally ripe for anything that should occasion romping and merriment, they had carried it into instant effect. The old housekeeper had been consulted; the antique clothespresses and wardrobes rummaged, and made to yield up the relics of finery that had not seen the light for several generations; the younger part of the company had been privately convened from the parlour and hall, and the whole had been bedizened out into a burlesque imitation of an antique mask.

Master Simon led the van, as "Ancient Christmas", quaintly apparelled in a ruff, a short cloak, which had very much the aspect of one of the old housekeeper's petticoats, and a hat that might have served for a village steeple, and must indubitably have figured in the days of the Covenanters. From under this his nose curved boldly forth flushed with a frostbitten bloom, that seemed the very trophy of a December blast. He was accompanied by the blue-eyed romp, dished up as "Dame Mince Pie", in the venerable magnificence of a faded brocade, long stomacher, peaked hat, and high heeled shoes. The rest of the train had been metamorphosed in various ways and the irruption of this motley crew, with beat of drum, according to ancient custom was the consummation of uproar and merriment. Master Simon covered himself with glory by the stateliness with which, as Ancient Christmas, he walked a minuet with the peerless, though giggling, Dame Mince Pie. It was followed by a dance of all the characters, which, from its medley of costumes, seemed as though the old family portraits had skipped down from their frames to join in the sport.

The worthy squire contemplated these fantastic sports, and this resurrection of his wardrobe, with the simple relish of childish delight. He stood chuckling and rubbing his hands, and scarcely hearing a word the parson said, notwithstanding that the latter was discoursing most authentically on the ancient and stately dance of the Paon, or peacock from which he conceived the minuet to be derived. For my part I was in a continual excitement, from the varied scenes of whim and innocent gaiety passing before me. It was inspiring to me to see wild-eyed frolic and warm-hearted hospitality breaking out from among the chills and glooms of the winter, and old age throwing off his apathy and catching once more the freshness of youthful enjoyment.

I felt also an interest in the scene, from the consideration that these fleeting customs were posting fast into oblivion, and that this was perhaps, the only family in England in which the whole of them were still punctiliously observed. There was a quaintness, too, mingled with all this revelry, that gave it a peculiar zest: it was suited to the time and place; and as the old manor-house almost reeled with mirth and wassail, it seemed echoing back the joviality of long-departed years.

A Christmas Scrapbook

Enter the Hero

WHY, GENTLEMEN, do you know what you do? ha! would you have kept me out? Christmas, old Christmas, Christmas of London, and Captain Christmas? Pray you, let me be brought before my lord chamberlain, I'll not be answered else: *'Tis merry in hall, when beards was all*: I have seen the time you have wish'd for me, for a merry Christmas; and now you have me, they would not let me in: *I must come another time!* a good jest, as if I could come more than once a year Why, I am no dangerous person, and so I told my friends of the guard. I am old Gregory Christmas still, and though I am come out of Pope's Head Alley, as good a Protestant as any in my parish.

FROM *A MASQUE OF CHRISTMAS* BY BEN JONSON (1616)

A Toast in Lamb's Wool

The Wassail Bowl was sometimes composed of ale instead of wine; with nutmeg, sugar, toast, ginger, and roasted crabs; in this way the nutbrown beverage is still prepared in some old families, and round the hearths of substantial farmers at Christmas. It is also called Lamb's Wool, and is celebrated by Herrick in his *Twelfth Night*:

> 'Next crowne the bowle full
> With gentle Lamb's Wool;
> Add sugar, nutmeg, and ginger,
> With store of ale too;
> And thus ye must doe
> To make the Wassaile a swinger.'

The custom of drinking out of the same cup gave place to each having his cup. When the steward came to the door with the Wassel, he was to cry three times, *Wassel, Wassel, Wassel*, and then the chappell (chaplein) was to answer with a song.

From *Archaeologia*

LET US BE GAY

> So now is come our joyfull'st feast;
> Let every man be jolly;
> Each room with ivy leaves is drest,
> And every post with holly.

George Wither (1585–1667)

BIRD SONG AT NIGHT

Some say that ever 'gainst that season comes
Wherein our Saviour's birth is celebrated,
The bird of dawning singeth all night long;
And then, they say, no spirit can walk abroad;
The nights are wholesome; then no planets strike,
No fairy takes, no witch hath power to charm;
So hallow'd and so gracious is the time.

William Shakespeare (1564–1616)

FROM MARMION

Heap on more wood! The wind is chill;
But let it whistle as it twill,
We'll keep our Christmas merry still…

England was merry England, when
Old Christmas brought his sports again.
'Twas Christmas broached the mightiest ale;
'Twas Christmas told the merriest tale;
A Christmas gambo; oft could cheer
The poor man's heart through half the year.

Sir Walter Scott (1771–1832)

YULETIDE SUPERSTITIONS

If one would go to the crossroads between eleven and twelve on Christmas Day, and listen, he would hear what most concerns him in the coming year.

On Christmas Eve thrash the garden with a flail, with only a shirt on, and the grass will grow well next year.

If a shirt be spun, woven and sewed by a pure, chaste maiden on Christmas Day, it will be proof against lead or steel.

If one is born at sermon time on Christmas morning, he will possess the power to see spirits.

The ashes of the Christmas log were supposed to give fertility to the ground, to rid cattle of vermin, to cure toothache and to protect the house from fire and ill-luck.

If a girl knocked loudly at the sty door on Christmas Eve and a great hog grunted in reply, her predestined husband would be an old man; if it was a little pig, that gave promise of a young one.

AIR MINISTRY, NOTE

If Christmas day on Thursday be,
A windy winter ye shall see,
Windy weather in each week,
And hard tempest strong and thick;
The summer shall be good and dry,
Corn and beasts shall multiply.

From an old almanack

USEFUL ADVICE

At Christmas play and make good cheer,

For Christmas comes but once a year.

At Christmas be merry and thank God for all,

And feast thy poor neighbour, the great with the small.

From *Hundreth Good Poyntes of Husbandrie* by Thomas
Tusser (1557)

SAUSAGE AND STRONG BEER

In English gentleman, at the opening of the great day (i.e.
on Christmas Day in the morning), had all his tenants and
neighbours enter his hall by daybreak. The strong beer
was broached, and the blackjacks went plentifully about
with toast, sugar, and nutmeg, and good Cheshire cheese.

The Hackin (the great sausage) must be boiled by daybreak or else two young men must take the maiden (i.e.
the cook) by the arms, and run her round the marketplace
till she is shamed of her laziness.

From *Round About Our Sea Coal Fire*

OLD CUSTOMS ARE BEST

In modern times mistletoe was abandoned in the Christmas decking of churches, together with kissing at the

services, because both were found to set the young ladies and gentlemen a-reading of the marriage service. Holly was substituted for the kisses and mistletoe, to indicate to them the dark monotony of matrimony and the numerous thorns with which it abounds.

FOR A CHRISTMAS CARD

Wake from thy nest, Robin-red-breast,
   Sing birds, in every furrow;
And from each hill, let music shrill
   Give my fair Love good-morrow!

Thomas Heywood (d. 1649)

PEACOCK PIE

The peacock was anciently in great demand for stately entertainments. Sometimes it was made into a pie, at one end of which the head appeared above the crust, in all its plumage, with the beak richly gilt; at the other end the tail was displayed. Such pies were served up at the solemn banquets of chivalry, when knights-errant pledged themselves to undertake any perilous enterprise; whence came the ancient oath, used by Justice Shallow, 'by cock and pie'.

The peacock was also an important dish for the Christmas feast; and Massinger, in his *City Madam*, gives some idea of the extravagance with which this, as well as other dishes, was prepared for the revels of an age which knew not 'rationing':

'Men may talk of country Christmasses:
Their thirty-pound butter'd eggs, their pies of carps' tongues,
Their pheasants drench'd with ambergris; the carcases
Of three fat wethers bruised for gravy, to
Make sauce for a single peacock; yet their feasts
Were fasts, compared with the city's.'

SNAPDRAGON

"This sport is seldom exhibited but in winter, and chiefly at Christmas time: it is simply heating of brandy, or some other ardent spirit, in a dish with raisins; when, the brandy being set on fire, the young folk of both sexes, standing round it, pluck; out the raisins, and eat them as hastily as they can, but rarely without burning their hands, or scolding their mouths" (Strutt). It is usual to extinguish the lights in the room while the game is in progress.

Alice, it will be remembered, encountered a *Snapdragonfly* through the looking-glass. Its body was 'made of plum-pudding, its wings of holly leaves and its head is a raisin burning in brandy'.

"And what does it live on?" Alice asked .

"Frumenty and mince pie . . . and it makes its nest in a Christmas box."

FROM *IN MEMORIAM*

The time draws near the birth of Christ;
 The moon is hid, the night is still;
 The Christmas bells from hill to hill
Answer each other in the mist.

But they my troubled spirit rule,
 For they controll'd me when a boy;
 They bring me sorrow touched with joy
The merry merry bells of Yule.

Alfred, Lord Tennyson (1809–1892)

A SALUTARY LESSON

In the Tyrolean Alps it is believed that the cattle have the gift of Language on Christmas Eve. But it is a sin to attempt to play the eavesdropper on them. An Alpine story is told of a farmer's servant who did not believe that the cattle could speak, and, to make sure, he hid in his master's stable on Christmas Eve and listened. When the clock struck twelve he was surprised at what he heard. "We shall have hard work; to do this day week," said one horse. "Yes, the farmer's servant is heavy," answered the other horse. "And the way to the churchyard is long and steep," said the first. The servant was buried that day week.

CHRISTMAS EVE

The minstrels played their Christmas tune
Tonight beneath my cottage eaves;
While smitten by a lofty moon,
The encircling laurels, thick with leaves,
Gave back a rich and dazzling sheen,
That overpowered their natural green!

William Wordsworth (1770–1850)

THE YULE LOG

The Yule clog is a great log of wood, sometimes the root of a tree, brought into the house with great ceremony, on Christmas Eve, laid in the fireplace, and lighted with the brand of last year's clog. While it lasted, there was great drinking, singing, and telling of tales. Sometimes it was accompanied by Christmas candles; the ruddy blaze of the great wood fire. The Yule clog was to burn all night; if it went out, it was considered a sign of ill-luck. Herrick mentions it in one of his songs:

'Come, bring with a noise,
My merrie, merrie boyes,
The Christmas log to the firing;
While my good dame, she
Bids ye all be free,
And drink to your heart's desiring.'

There were several superstitions connected with it among the peasantry. If a squinting person come to the house while it was burning, or a person barefooted, it was considered an ill-omen. The brand remaining from the Yule clog was carefully put away to light the next year's Christmas fire.

SONG FOR MERRY CHRISTMAS

Now Christmas soon will come again,
    And everybody knows it,
Make yourself merry while you can,
    If you have the means to do it.
I'll tell you of things what you may see,
    When you're about the town,
And if you have got any money to spend
    I hope you'll lay out a brown—brown
        —brown.

Now Christmas as it will soon arrive,
   Let's hope each hungry sinner,
Will have a good big lump of beef,
   And a pudding for his dinner.

Street Ballad (early 19th century)

DISSENTIENT VOICE

Glorious time of great too much!
Too much heat and too much noise,
Too much babblement of boys,
Too much eating, too much drinking,
Too much everything but thinking.

Leigh Hunt (1784–1859)

ONCE UPON A TIME

A man might then behold
   At Christmas, in each hall,
Good fires to curb the cold,
   And meat for great and small.
The neighbours were friendly bidden
   And all had welcome true,
The poor from the gates were not chidden,
   When this old cap was new.

Thomas Hood (1779-1845)

CAROL

I sing of a maiden
That is makéles:
King of all kings
To her son she chés.

He came al so stillé
There his moder was,
As dew in Aprillé
That falleth on the grass.

He came al so stillé
To his moderes bour,
As dew in Aprillé
That falleth on the flour.

He came al so stillé
There his moder lay,
As dew in Aprillé
That falleth on the spray.

Moder and maiden
Was never none but she:
Well may such a lady
Godé's moder be.

Anonymous (14th century)

ALL THAT REMAINS

But is old, old, good old Christmas gone? Nothing but the hair of his good, grey, old head and beard left? Well, I will have that, seeing I cannot have more of him.

Hue and Cry after Christmas

WHAT WILLIE WANTS

Dear Santa Claus
You bought me a sled
To me a year ago
And when you come again I hope
You'll bring along some snow

Anon

CHRISTMAS MORNINGS

LEONARD CLARK

UP IN the morning early
sunlight on the cold floor,
nobody singing on far hills,
animals quite, something in the air,
a touch of frost on the window sills.
a father standing by the door,
a mother smiling there,
a baby sleeping in the morning early.

Up in the morning, early
firelight on the warm floor,
everybody singing on the near hills,
whole house alive, something in the air,
a lick of rain on the window sills,
father standing by the door,
mother laughing there,
me waking in the morning early.

CHRISTMAS DAY

NORA PERRY

HAT'S THE hurry, what's this flurry,
   All throughout the house today?
Everywhere a merry scurry.
   Everywhere a sound of play.
Something, too, 's the matter, matter,
   Out-of-doors as well as in,
For the bell goes clatter, clatter,
   Every minute—such a din!

Go and ask *them* what's the matter,
   What the fun outside and in—
What the meaning of the clatter,
   What the bustle and the din.
Hear them, hear them laugh and shout then,
   All together hear them say,
"Why, what have you been about, then,
   Not to know it's Christmas day?"

THE LITTLE MATCH-GIRL

HANS CHRISTIAN ANDERSEN

T WAS dreadfully cold, it was snowing fast, and almost dark; the evening—the last evening of the old year—was drawing in. But, cold and dark as it was, a poor little girl, with bare head and feet, was still wandering about the streets When she left her home she had slippers on, but they were much too large for her—indeed, properly, they belonged to her mother, and had dropped off her feet whilst she was running very fast across the road, to get out of the way of two carriages. One of the slippers was not to be found; the other had been snatched up by a little boy, who ran off with it.

So the little girl now walked on, her bare feet quite red and blue with the cold. She carried a small bundle of matches in her hand, and a good many more in her tattered apron. No one had bought any of them the live-long day—no one had given her a single penny. Trembling with cold and hunger, she crept on, the picture of sorrow.

The snowflakes fell on her long, fair hair, which curled in pretty ringlets over her shoulders; but she thought not of her own beauty, or of the cold. Lights were glimmering through every window, and the savour of roast goose reached her from several houses; it was New Year's eve, and it was of this that she thought.

In a corner formed by two houses, one of which projected beyond the other, she sat down, drawing her little feet close under her, but in vain she could not warm them. She dared not go home, she had sold no matches, earned not a single penny, and perhaps her father would beat her; besides, her home was almost as cold as the street—it was an attic; and, although the larger of the many chinks in the roof were stopped up with straw and rags, the wind and snow often penetrated through. Her hands were nearly dead with cold; one little match from her bundle would warm them, perhaps, if she dared light it. She drew one out, and struck it against the wall. It was a bright warm flame, and she held her hands over it. It was quite an illumination for that poor little girl, nay, call it rather a magic taper, for it seemed to her as though she were sitting before a large iron stove with brass ornaments. So beautifully blazed the fire within that the child stretched out her feet to warm them also. Alas! in an instant the flame had died away, the stove vanished, the little girl sat cold and comfortless, with the burnt match in her hand.

A second match was struck against the wall, it kindled and blazed, and wherever its light fell the wall became transparent as a veil—the little girl could see into the room within. She saw the table spread with a snow-like damask cloth, whereon were ranged shining china dishes.

The roast goose stuffed with apples and dried plums stood at one end, smoking hot, and—which was pleasantest of all to see—the goose, with knife and fork still in her breast, jumped down from the dish, and waddled along the floor right up to the poor child. The match was burnt out, and only the thick, hard wall was beside her.

She kindled a third match. Again shot up the flame;— and now she was sitting under a most beautiful Christmas-tree, far larger, and far more prettily decked out than the one she had seen last Christmas-eve through the glass doors of the rich merchant's house. Hundreds of wax-tapers lighted up the green branches, and tiny painted figures, such as she had seen in the shop windows, looked down from the tree upon her. The child stretched out her hands towards them in delight, and in that moment the light of the match was quenched. Still, however, the Christmas candles burned higher and higher—she beheld them beaming like stars in heaven. One of them fell, the light streaming behind it like a long, fiery tail.

"Now some one is dying," said the little girl softly, for she had been told by her old grandmother—the only person who had ever been kind to her, and who was now dead—that when ever a star falls an immortal spirit returns to the God who gave it. She struck yet another match against the wall, it flamed up, and, surrounded by its light, appeared before her that same dear grandmother, gentle and loving as always, but bright and happy as she had never looked during her lifetime.

"Grandmother!" exclaimed the child, "oh, take me with you! I know you will leave me as soon as the match goes out—you will vanish like the warm fire in the stove, like the splendid New Year's feast, like the beautiful large Christmas-tree," and she hastily lighted all the remaining matches in the bundle, lest her grandmother should disappear. And the matches burned with such a blaze of splendour, that noon-day could scarcely have been brighter. Never had the good old grandmother looked so tall and stately, so beautiful and kind. She took the little girl in her arms, and they both flew together—joyfully and gloriously they flew—higher and higher, till they were in that place where neither cold, nor hunger, nor pain is ever known—they were in Paradise.

But in the cold morning hour, crouching in the corner of the wall, the poor little girl was found—her cheeks glowing, her lips smiling—frozen to death on the last night of the Old Year. The New Year's sun shone on the lifeless child; motionless she sat there with the matches in her lap, one bundle of them quite burnt out.

"She has been trying to warm herself, poor thing!" the people said; but no one knew of the sweet visions she had beheld, or how gloriously she and her grandmother were celebrating their New Year's festival.

The Little Match Girl

Christmas Day in Bunnyland

CHRISTMAS DAY IN BUNNYLAND

ADA LEONORA HARRIS

CHILDREN LOVE a Christmas Tree;
  Lighted up they think it's grand!
So 't is right that there should be
Christmas trees in Bunnyland.

How they fuss and bustle till
  All is ready for the day!
Then the little Bunnies will
  Stamp their feet and cry "Hooray!"

But some Rabbits there may be
  Who've no money to buy toys
For a proper Christmas tree
  For their little girls and boys.

So, if you've a toy to spare,
  Do not tell a single soul,
Wrap it up and then with care
  Drop it down a Rabbit hole.

Now Thrice Welcome Christmas

ANON

Now thrice welcome, Christmas,
  Which brings us good cheer,
Minc'd pies and plum porridge,
  Good ale and strong beer;
With pig, goose, and capon,
  The best that can be,
So well doth the weather
  And our stomachs agree.

Observe how the chimneys
  Do smoke all about,
The cooks are providing
  For dinner no doubt;
For those on whose table
  No victuals appear,
O may they keep Lent
  All the rest of the year!

With holly and ivy
   So green and so gay,
We deck up our houses
   As fresh as the day,
With bays and rosemary,
   And laurel complete;
And every one now
   Is a king in conceit.

THE CHRISTMAS CUCKOO

ONCE UPON a time there stood in the midst of a bleak moor, in the north country, a certain village. All its people were poor, for their fields were barren, and they had little trade; but the poorest of them all were two brothers called Scrub and Spare. They were cobblers, and had but one stall between them. It was a hut built of clay and wattles. The door was low and always open, for there was no window. The roof did not entirely keep out the rain, and the only thing with any look of comfort about it was a wide hearth, for which the brothers could never find wood enough to make a good fire. There they worked in most brotherly friendship, though the people did not give them very many shoes to make or mend.

The people of that village did not need many shoes, and better cobblers than Scrub and Spare might be found. Spiteful people said there were no shoes so bad that they would not be worse for their mending. Nevertheless Scrub and Spare managed to live by means of their own trade, a small barley field, and cottage garden, till a new cobbler arrived in the village. He had lived in the chief city of the kingdom, and, by his own account, cobbled for the Queen and the princesses. His awls were sharp and his lasts were new. He set up his stall in a neat cottage with two windows.

The villagers soon found out that one patch of his would outwear two of the brothers'. In short, all the mending left Scrub and Spare, and went to the new cobbler. The season had been wet and cold, their barley did not ripen well, and the cabbages never half closed in the garden. So the brothers were poor that winter; and when Christmas came, they had nothing to feast on but a barley loaf, a piece of musty bacon, and some small beer of their own brewing.

Worse than that, the snow was very deep, and they could get no firewood. Their hut stood at the end of the village; beyond it spread the bleak moor, now all white and silent. But that moor had once been a forest. Great roots or old trees were still to be found in it, loosened from the soil and laid bare by the winds and rains. One of these, a rough, heavy log, lay close to their door, the half of it above the snow.

Spare said to his brother: "Shall we sit here cold on Christmas Day while the great root lies yonder? Let us chop it up for firewood, the work will make us warm."

"No," said Scrub; "it's not right to chop wood on Christmas. Besides, that root is too hard to be cut with any axe."

"Hard or not, we must have a fire," replied Spare. "Come, brother, help me in with it. Poor as we are, there is nobody in the village will have such a Yule log as our's."

Scrub liked to be a little grand sometimes, and in hopes of having a fine Yule log, both brothers strove with all their might till, between pulling and pushing, the great old root was safe on the hearth, and soon began to crackle and blaze with the red embers. In high glee, the cobblers sat down to their beer and bacon. The door was shut, for there was nothing but cold moonlight and snow outside. But the hut, strewn with fir branches and decked with holly, looked cheerful as the ruddy blaze flared up and made their hearts glad.

"Long life and good fortune to ourselves, brother!" said Spore. "I hope you will drink that toast, and may we never have a worse fire on Christmas—but what is that?"

Spare set down the drinking-horn, a the brothers listened in great surprise, for out of the blazing root they heard "Cuckoo! Cuckoo!" as plain as ever the spring bird's voice came over the moor on a May morn.

"It is something bad," said Scrub, very much frightened.

"Maybe not," said Spare.

And out of the deep hole at the side which the fire had not reached flew a large grey cuckoo, and alighted on the table before them. Much as the cobblers had been surprised at first, they were still more so when the bird began to speak.

"Good gentlemen," said the cuckoo, "what season is this?"

"It's Christmas," replied Spare.

"Then a merry Christmas to you!" said the cuckoo. "I went to sleep in the hollow of that old root tree last summer and never woke till the heat of your fire made me think it was summer again. But now, since you have burned my lodging, let me stay in your hut till the spring comes round—I only want a hole to sleep in, and when I go on my travels next summer you may be sure I will bring you some gift for your trouble."

"Stay, and welcome," said Spare, while Scrub sat wondering if it were something bad or not. "I'll make you a good warm hole in the thatch. But you must be hungry after that long sleep. There is a slice of barley bread. Come, help us to keep Christmas!"

The cuckoo ate up the slice, drank some water from the Brown jug—for it would take no beer—and flew into a snug hole which Spare scooped for it in the thatch of the hut.

Scrub said he was afraid the bird wouldn't be lucky. But as it slept on, and the days passed, he forgot his fears. So the snow melted, the heavy rains came, the cold grew less, and the days became longer; and one sunny morning the brothers were awakened by the cuckoo shouting its own cry to let them know the spring had come.

"Now," said the bird, "I am going on my travels over the world to tell men of the spring. There is no country where trees bud, or flowers bloom, that I will not cry in before the year goes round. Give me another slice of bread to keep me on my journey, and tell me what gift I shall bring you at the end of the twelve months."

Scrub would have been angry with his brother for cutting so large a slice, their store of barley meal being low; but his mind was so taken up with what present it would be best for him to ask. At length a lucky thought struck him.

"Good Master Cuckoo," said he, "if a great traveller who sees all the world like you, could know of any place where diamonds or pearls were to be found, one of a fairly large size brought in your beak would help such poor men as my brother and me to get something better than barley to give bread to give you the next time you come."

"I know nothing of diamonds or pearls," said the cuckoo. "They are in the hearts of rocks and the sands in the rivers. I know only of that which grows on the earth. But there are two trees close by the well that lies at the end of the world. One of them is called the golden tree, for its leaves are all beaten gold. Every winter they fall into the well with a sound like that of scattered gold, and I know not what becomes of them. As for the other, it is always green, like a laurel. Some call it the wise, and some the merry tree. Its leaves never fall but they that get one of them keep a cheerful heart in spite of all troubles, and can make themselves merry in a hut as in a palace."

"Good Master Cuckoo, bring me a leaf off that tree!" cried Spare.

"Now, brother, don't be a fool!" said Scrub. "Think of the leaves of gold. Dear Master Cuckoo, bring me one of them!"

Before another word could be said, the cuckoo had flown out of the open door, and was shouting its spring cry over moor and meadow.

The brothers were poorer than ever that year. Nobody sent them a single shoe to mend. The new cobbler said, in scorn, they should come over and work for him. Scrub and Spare would have left the village but for their barley field, their cabbage garden, and a maid called Fairfeather, whom both the cobblers had courted for seven years without even knowing whom she meant to favour.

Sometimes Fairfeather seemed to favour Scrub, sometimes she smiled on Spare; but the brothers were always friends and did not quarrel. They sowed their barley, planted their cabbage, and, now their trade was gone, worked in the fields of some of the rich villagers to make a scanty living.

So the seasons came and passed. Spring, Summer, harvest, and winter followed each other as they have always done. At the end of the winter Scrub and Spare had grown so poor and ragged that Fairfeather thought them beneath her notice. Old neighbours forgot to invite them to wedding feasts or merrymaking. They thought the cuckoo had forgotten them too, when at daybreak, on the first of April, they heard a hard beak knocking at their door and a voice crying:

"Cuckoo! cuckoo! let me in with my gifts."

Spare ran to open the door, and in came the cuckoo carrying on one side of his bill a golden leaf larger than that of any tree in the north country; and in the other, one like that of the common laurel, only it had a fresher green.

"Here," it said, giving the gold to Scrub and the green to Spare; "it is a long way to carry them from the end of the world. Give me a slice of bread, for I must tell the north country that the spring has come."

Scrub did not grudge the thickness of that slice, it was cut from their last loaf.

So much gold had never been in the cobbler's hands before, and he could not help exulting over his brother.

"See the wisdom of my choice!" he said, holding up the large leaf of gold. "As for yours, as good might be plucked from any hedge. I wonder such a wise bird would carry the like so far."

"Good Master Cobbler," cried the cuckoo, finishing the slice, "your words are more hasty than kind. If your brother is disappointed this time, I go on the same journey every year, and for your kind treatment will think it no trouble to bring each of you whichever leaf you wish."

"Darling cuckoo!" cried Scrub, "bring me a golden one."

And Spare, looking up from the green leaf on which he gazed as though it were a crown jewel, said:

"Be sure to bring me one from the merry tree."

And away flew the cuckoo once again.

"'This is the Feast of All Fools , and it ought to be your birthday," said Scrub.

"Did ever man fling away such a chance of becoming rich! Much good your merry leaves will do when you are so poor!"

So he went no; but Spare laughed at him, and answered with many old proverbs about the cares that come with gold, till Scrub, at length growing angry, vowed his brother was not fit to live with a gentleman like himself. And taking his lasts, his awls, and his golden leaf, he left the wattle hut and went to tell the villagers.

They were surprised at the folly of Spare, and charmed with Scrub's good sense, more so when he showed them the golden leaf, and told that the cuckoo would bring him one every spring. The new cobbler at once made him a partner. The greatest people sent him their shoes to mend. Fairfeather smiled kindly on him, and in the course of the summer they were married, with a grand wedding feast, at which the whole village danced, except Spare, who was not invited, because the bride said he was low-minded, and his brother thought he was a disgrace to the family.

Indeed, all who heard the story thought that Spare must be mad, and nobody would take up with him but a lame tinker, a beggar boy, and a poor woman who was looked as a witch because she was old and ugly. As for Scrub, he went with Fairfeather to a cottage close by that of the new cobbler, and quite as fine. There he mended shoes so as to please everyone, had a scarlet coat for holidays, and a fat goose for dinner every wedding-day. Fairfeather, too, had a crimson gown and fine blue ribbons. But neither she nor Scrub were content, for to buy all these grand things the golden leaf had to be broken and parted with piece by piece, so the last morsel was gone before the cuckoo came with another.

Spare lived on in the old hut, and worked in the cabbage garden. (Scrub had got the barley field, because he was the elder.) Every day his coat grew more ragged, and the hut more weather-beaten, but the people remarked that he never looked sad nor sour. The wonder was, that from the time they began to keep his company, the tinker grew kinder to the ass with which he travelled the country, the beggar boy kept out of mischief, and the old woman was never cross to her cat or angry with the children.

Every first of April the cuckoo came tapping at their doors with the golden leaf to Scrub and the green to Spare. Fairfeather would have treated him nobly with wheaten bread and honey, for she had some notion of trying to make him bring two gold leaves instead of one. But the cuckoo flew away to eat barley bread with Spare, saying he was not fit company for fine people, and liked the old hut where he slept so snugly from Christmas to Spring.

Scrub spent the golden leaves, and Spare kept the merry ones; and I know not how many years passed in this manner, when a great lord, who owned the village came to dwell near. His castle stood on the moor. It was old and strong, with high towers and a deep moat. All the country as far as one could see from the highest turret belonged to this lord; but he had not been there for twenty years, and would not have come then, only he was very sad.

The cause of his grief was that he had been Prime Minister at Court, and in high favour, till somebody told the Crown Prince that he had spoken With great disrespect about the turning out of His Royal Highness's toes, and the king that he did not lay on taxes enough; whereon the north country lord was turned out of office and sent to his own estate. There he lived for some weeks in very bad temper. The servants said nothing would please him, and the people of the village put on their worst clothes lest he should raise their rents. But one day, in the harvest time, his lordship chanced to meet Spare gathering watercresses at a meadow stream, and fell into talk with the cobbler.

How it was nobody could tell, but from that hour the great lord cast away his sadness. He forgot his lost office and his Court enemies, the King's taxes and the Crown Prince's toes, and went about with a noble train, hunting, fishing, and making merry in his hall, where all travellers were well treated and all the poor were welcome.

This strange story soon spread through the north country, and a great company came to the cobbler's hut—rich men who had lost their money, poor men who had lost their friends, beauties who had grown old, wits who had gone out of fashion—all came to talk with Spare, and whatever their troubles had been, all went home merry.

The rich gave him presents, the poor gave him thanks. Spare's coat was no longer ragged, he had bacon with his cabbage, and the people of the village began to think there was some sense in him after all.

By this time his fame had reached the chief city of the kingdom, and even the Court. There were a great many discontented people there besides the King, who had lately fallen into ill humour because a princess, who lived in a kingdom near his own, and who had seven islands for her dowry, would not marry his eldest son. So a royal page was sent to Spare, with a velvet cloak, a diamond ring, and a command that he should come to the Court at once.

"Tomorrow is the first of April," said Spare, "and I will go with you two hours after sunrise."

The page lodged all night at the castle, and the cuckoo came at sunrise with the merry leaf.

"The Court is a fine place," he said, when the cobbler told him he was going. "But I cannot come there, they would lay snares and catch me. So be careful of the leaves I have brought you, and give me a farewell slice of barley bread."

Spare was sorry to part with the cuckoo, little as he had of his company. But he gave him a slice which would have broken Scrub's heart in the former times, it was so large. And having sewed up the leaves in the lining of his leather doublet, he set out with the page on his way to court.

His coming caused great surprise there. Everybody wondered what the king could see in such a common-man. But hardly had His Majesty talked with him half an hour, when the princess and her seven islands were forgotten, and orders given that a feast for all-comers should be spread in the large dining-hall

The princess of the blood, the great lords and ladies, the ministers of State, and the judges of the land had a talk with Spare; the more they talked the lighter grew their hearts, so that such changes had never been seen at Court. The lords forgot their spites and ladies their envies, the princes and Ministers made friends among themselves, and judges showed no favour.

As for Spare, he had a room set apart for him in the palace, and a seat at the King's table. One sent him rich robes and another costly jewels. But in the midst of all his greatness he still wore the leathern doublet, which the palace servants thought very mean. One day the King's attention being drawn to it by the chief page, he asked why spare didn't give it to a beggar.

But the cobbler answered: "High and mighty King, this doublet was with me before silk and velvet came. I find it easier to wear than the court cut. Moreover, it serve to keep me humble, by recalling the days when it was my holiday dress."

The King thought this was a wise speech, and gave orders that no one should find fault with the leathern doublet. So things went on, till news of his brother's good fortune reached Scrub in the moorland cottage on another first of April, when the cuckoo came with two golden leaves because he had none to carry for Spare.

"Think of that!" said Fairfeather. "Here we are spending our lives in this humdrum place, and Spare making his fortune at the court with two or three paltry green leaves! What would they say to our golden ones? Let us pack up and make our way to the king's palace. I am sure he will honour, not to speak of all the fine clothes and presents we shall have."

Scrub thought there was a great deal in what his wife said, and they began to pack up. But it was soon found that there were very few things in the cottage fit for carrying to the Court. Fairfeather could not think of her wooden bowls, spoons, and plates being seen there. Scrub thought his lasts and awls had better be left behind, as without them no one would suspect him of being a cobbler. So, putting on their holiday clothes, Fairfeather took her looking-glass, and Scrub his drinking-horn, and each carrying a golden leaf wrapped up with great care that none might see it till they reached the palace, the pair set out with high hopes.

How far Scrub and Fairfeather journeyed I cannot say; but when the sun was high and warm at noon, they came into a wood both tired and hungry.

Letting in the New Year

"Husband," said Fairfeather, "you should not have such means thoughts. How can one eat barley bread on the way to a palace? Let us rest ourselves under this tree, and look at leaves to see if they are safe."

In looking at the leaves, and talking of what they were going to do when they came to the Court, Scrub and Fairfeather did not see that a very thin old woman had slipped from behind a tree, with a long staff in her hand and a great bag by her side.

"Noble lord and lady," she said,—"for I know you are such by your voices, though my eyes are dim and my hearing none of the sharpest,—will you tell me where I may find some water to mix a bottle of mead which I carry in my bag, because it is too strong for me?"

As the old woman spoke, she pulled out of her bag a large wooden bottle such as shepherds used in the olden times, corked with leaves rolled together, and having a small wooden cup hanging from its handle.

"Perhaps you will do me the favour to taste it," she said. "It is only made of the best of honey. I have also cream cheese and a wheaten loaf here, if such noble persons as you eat the like."

Scrub and Fairfeather were now sure, after this speech, that there must be about them something of the look that noble persons have. Besides, they were very hungry; and having with great haste wrapped up the golden leaves, they told the old woman that they were not at all proud, notwithstanding the lands and castles they had left behind them in the north country, and would willingly help to lighten the bag. The old woman would hardly sit down beside them she was humble and modest, but at length she did; and before the bag was half empty, Scrub and Fairfeather firmly believed that there must be something very noble-looking about them.

The old woman was a wood-witch. Her name was Buttertongue, and all her time was spent in making mead, which being boiled with strange herbs and spells, had the power of making all who drank it fall asleep and dream with their eyes open. She had two dwarfs of sons; one was named Spy and the other Pounce. Wherever their mother went, they were not far behind; and whoever tasted her mead was sure to be robbed by the dwarfs.

Scrub and Fairfeather sat leaning against the old tree. The cobbler had a lump of cheese in his hand; his wife held fast a hunch of bread. Their eyes and mouths were both open, but they were dreaming of the fine things at the Court, when the old woman raised her shrill voice:

"What ho, my sons! come here, and carry home the harvest."

No sooner had she spoken than the two little dwarfs darted out of the nearest thicket.

"Idle boys!" cried the mother, "what have you done to-day to help our living?"

"I have been to the city," said Spy, "and could see nothing. These are hard times for us—everybody minds his work so contentedly since that cobbler came. But here is a leathern doublet which his page threw out of the window. It's of no use but I brought it to let you see I was not idle." And he tossed down Spare's doublet, with the merry leaves in it, which he had carried like a bundle on his little back.

To let you know how Spy got hold of it, I must tell you that the forest was not far from the great city where Spare lived in such high esteem. All things had gone well with the cobbler till the King thought that it was quite unbecoming to see such a worthy man without a servant. His Majesty, therefore, to let all men understand his royal favour towards Spare, appointed one of his; own pages to wait upon him.

The name of this youth was Tinseltoes, and, though he was the seventh of the King's pages in rank, nobody in the Court had grander notions. Nothing could please him that had not gold or silver about it, and his grandmother feared he would hang himself for being made page to a cobbler. As for Spare, if anything could have troubled him, this mark of His majesty's kindness would have done it.

The honest man had been so used to serve himself that the page was always in the way; but his merry leaves came to his aid; and, to the great surprise of his grandmother, Tinseltoes took to the new service in a wonderful way. Some said it was because Spare gave him nothing to do but play at bowls all day on the palace green. Yet one thing vexed the heart of Tinseltoes, and that was his master's leathern doublet. But for it, he was sure people would never remember that Spare had been a cobbler; and the page took a deal of pains to let him see how much out of the fashion it was at the Court. But Spare answered Tinseltoes as he had done the King; and at last, finding nothing in, better would do, the page got up one fine morning earlier than his master, and tossed the leathern doublet out of the back window into a lane, where Spy found it and brought it to his mother.

"That nasty thing!" said the old woman. "Where is the good in it?"

By this time, Pounce had taken everything, of value from Scrub and Fairfeather—the looking-glass, the silver-rimmed horn, the husbands scarlet coat, the wife's gay cloak and, above all, the golden leaves, which so gladdened the hearts of old Buttertongue and her sons, that they threw the leathern doublet over the sleeping cobbler for a joke, and went off to their hut in the middle of the forest.

The sun was going down when Scrub and Fairfeather awoke from dreaming that they had been made a lord and a lady, and sat clothed in silk and velvet, feasting with the King in his palace hall. They were greatly disappointed to find their golden leaves and all their best things gone. Scrub tore his hair, and vowed to take the old woman's life, while Fairfeather uttered loud cries of sorrow. But Scrub, feeling cold for want of his coat, put on the leathern doublet without asking or caring whence it came.

Hardly was it buttoned on when a change came over him. He began to talk so merrily, that, instead of crying, Fairfeather made the wood ring with laughter. Both busied themselves in getting up a hut of branches, in which Scrub kindled a fire with a flint and steel, which, together with his pipe, he had brought unknown to Fairfeather, who had told him the like was never heard of at the Court. Then they found a Pheasant's nest at the root of an old oak, made a meal of roasted eggs, and went to sleep on a heap of long green grass which they had gathered, with nightingales singing all night long in the old trees about them.

So it happened that Scrub and Fairfeather stayed day after day in the forest, making their hut larger and more cosy against the winter, living on wild birds' eggs and berries, and never thinking of their lost golden leaves, or their journey to the Court.

In the meantime Spare missed his doublet. Tinseltoes, of course said he knew nothing about it. The whole palace was searched, and every servant questioned, till all the Court wondered why such a fuss was made about an old leathern doublet. That very day, things came back to their old fashion. Quarrels began among, the lords, and envies among the ladies. The King said his people did not pay him half enough taxes, the Queen wanted more Jewels, the servants took to their old quarrels and got up some new ones.

Spare found himself getting strangely dull, and very

much out of place. Nobles began to ask what business a cobbler had at the King's table, and His Majesty ordered the palace records to find out if such a thing had ever taken place before. The cobbler was too wise to tell all he had lost with that doublet; but as by this time he knew the Court customs, he offered a reward of fifty gold pieces to anyone who would bring him news about it.

Scarcely was this made known in the city, when the gates and outer courts of the palace were filled with men, women, and children—some bringing leathern doublets of every cut and colour, some with tales of what they had heard and seen in their walks round about the palace. So much news about all sorts of great people came out of these stories, that lords and ladies ran to complain of Spare as one who spoke against people. His Majesty, being now sure that there was no example in all the palace records of such a retainer, sent forth a decree sending the cobbler away for ever from the Court, and giving all his goods to the page Tinseltoes.

That royal decree was hardly issued before the page had taken for himself Spare's rich room, his costly garments, and all the presents the people at the Court had given him. While Spare, having no longer the fifty pieces of gold to give, was glad to make his escape out of a back window, for fear of the nobles, who vowed to have revenge on him, and the crowd, who were ready to stone him for cheating them about his doublet.

The window from which spare let himself down with a

strong rope, was that from which Tinseltoes had tossed the doublet; and as the cobbler came down late in the twilight, a poor woodman, with a heavy load of fagots, stopped and stared at him in great surprise.

"What is the matter, friend?" asked Spare. "Did you never see a man coming down from a back window before?"

"Why," said the woodman, "the last morning I passed here, a leathern doublet came out of that very window, and I feel sure you are the owner of it."

"That I am, friend," said the cobbler eagerly. "Can you tell me which way that doublet went?"

"As I walked on," said the woodman, "a dwarf, called Spy, bundled it up and ran off to his mother in the forest."

"Honest friend," said Spare, taking off the last of his fine clothes (a grass-green cloak edged with gold), "I will give you this if you will follow the dwarf and bring me back my doublet."

'I t would not be good to carry fagots in," said the woodman. "But if you want back your doublet, the road to the forest lies at the end of this lane;" and he trudged away.

Having made up his doublet, and sure that neither crowd nor nobles could catch him in the forest, Spare went on his way, and was soon among the tall trees; but neither hut nor dwarf could he see. Moreover, the night came on; the wood was dark and thick, but here and there the moon shone through its lanes, the great owls flitted about, and the nightingales sang. So he went on, hoping to find some place of shelter.

At last the red light of a fire, shining through a thicket, led him to the door of a low hut. It stood half open, as if there was nothing to fear, and within he saw his brother Scrub snoring loudly on a bed of grass, at the foot of which lay his own leathern doublet; while Fairfeather, in a dress made of plaited rushes, sat roasting pheasants' eggs by the fire.

"Good evening, mistress!" said Spare stepping in.

The blaze shone on him, but so changed was her brother-in-law with his Court life, that Fairfeather did not know him, and she answered far more kindly than was her wont.

"Good evening, master! Whence come you so late? but speak low, for my good man has tired himself cutting wood, and is taking a sleep, as you see, before supper."

"A good rest to him!" said Spare, seeing he was not known. "I come from the Court for a day's hunting, and have lost my way in the forest."

"Sit down and have a share of our supper," said Fairfeather, "I will put on some more eggs in the ashes; and tell me the news of Court—I used to think of it long ago when I was young and foolish."

"Did you never go there?" said the cobbler.

"So fair a dame as you would make the ladies wonder."

"You are pleased to flatter," said Fair feather; "but my husband has a brother there, and we left our moorland village to try our fortune also. An old woman at the entrance to this forest, by means of fair words, got us to take some strong drink, which caused us to fall asleep and dream of great things. But when we woke, everything had been robbed from us—my looking-glass, my scarlet cloak, my husband's Sunday coat; and, in place of all, the robbers left behind him that old doublet, which he has worn ever since, and he never was so merry in all his life, though we live in this poor hut."

"It is a shabby doublet, that," said Spare, taking up the garment, and seeing that it was his own, for the merry leaves were still sewed in its lining. "it would be good for hunting in, however—your husband would be glad to part with it, I dare say, in exchange for the handsome cloak;" and he pulled off the green mantle and buttoned on the doublet, much to Fairfeather's delight, who ran and shook Scrub, crying: "Husband, husband, rise and see what a good bargain I have made!"

Scrub gave one last snore, and muttered something about the root being hard. But he rubbed his eyes, gazed up at his brother and said:

"Spare, is that really you? How did you like the Court, and have you made your fortune?"

"That I have, brother," said Spare, "in getting back my own good leathern doublet. Come, let us eat eggs, and rest ourselves here this night. In the morning we will return to our own old hut, at the end of the moorland village, where the Christmas Cuckoo will come and bring us leaves."

Scrub and Fairfeather agreed. So in the morning they all returned, and found the old hut little the worse for wear and weather. The people of the village came about them to ask news of Court, and see if they had made their fortune. Everybody was surprised to find the three poorer than ever, but somehow they liked to go to the hut. Spare brought out the lasts and awls he had hidden in the corner. Scrub and he began their old trade again, and the whole north country found out that there never were such cobblers.

They mended the shoes of the lords and ladies as well as the common people; everybody was pleased with the work. Their trade grew greater from day to day, and all that were discontented or unlucky came to the hut as in old times, before Spare went to the Court.

The rich brought presents, the poor did them service. The hut itself changed no one knew how. Flowering honeysuckle grew over its roof; red and white roses grew thick about its door. Moreover, the Christmas Cuckoo always came on the first of April, bringing three leaves of the merry tree—for Scrub and Fairfeather would have no more golden ones. So it was with them when I last heard the news of the north country.

The Holly and the Ivy

TRADITIONAL

THE HOLLY and the ivy,
When they are both full grown,
Of all the trees that are in the wood,
The holly bears the crown.

O the rising of the sun,
And the running of the deer,
The playing of the merry organ,
Sweet singing in the choir.

The holly bears a blossom,
As white as the lily flower,
And Mary bore sweet Jesus Christ,
To be our sweet Saviour.

The holly bears a berry,
As red as any blood,
And Mary bore sweet Jesus Christ,
To do poor sinners good.

The holly bears a prickle,
As sharp as any thorn,
And Mary bore sweet Jesus Christ,
On Christmas Day in the morn.

The holly bears a bark,
As bitter as any gall,
And Mary bore sweet Jesus Christ,
For to redeem us all.

O the rising of the sun,
And the running of the deer,
The playing of the merry organ,
Sweet singing in the choir.

HARK! THE HERALD ANGELS SING

CHARLES WESLEY

HARK THE herald angels sing,
Glory to the new-born King.
Peace on earth, and mercy mild,
God and sinners reconciled.
Joyful, all you nations rise,
Join the triumph of the skies.
With the angelic hosts proclaim,
"Christ is born in Bethlehem."

Hark! the herald angels sing,
"Glory to the new-born King."

Christ, by highest heaven adored,
Christ, the everlasting Lord.
Late in time behold him come,
Offspring of a Virgin's womb.
Veiled in flesh the Godhead see;
Hail the Incarnate Deity,
Pleased as Man with man to dwell,
Jesus our Emmanuel!

Hark! the herald angels sing,
"Glory to the new-born King."

Hail, the heaven-born Prince of Peace!
Hail, The Sun of Righteousness!
Light and life to all he brings,
Risen with healing in his wings.
Mild he lays his glory by,
Born that man no more may die,
Born to raise the sons of earth,
Born to give them second birth.

Hark! the herald angels sing,
"Glory to the new-born King."

LETTING IN THE NEW YEAR

HEAR THE clocks striking, one by one,
Twelve solemn strokes. The year is done.
Open the door and let us hear
The bells that welcome the new year.

Just fancy, sitting up so late!
But we were all allowed to wait
Until the poor old year was done,
And a nice new one had begun.